OXFORD STUDENT TEXTS

Series Editor: Victor Lee

✳

Geoffrey Chaucer

The Miller's Tale

Edited by
Dr Peter Mack and Chris Walton

OXFORD
UNIVERSITY PRESS

OXFORD
UNIVERSITY PRESS

Great Clarendon Street, Oxford OX2 6DP

Oxford University Press is a department of the University of Oxford.
It furthers the University's objective of excellence in research, scholarship,
and education by publishing worldwide in

Oxford New York

Auckland Bangkok Buenos Aires Cape Town
Chennai Dar es Salaam Delhi Hong Kong Istanbul Karachi
Kolkata Kuala Lumpur Madrid Melbourne Mexico City Mumbai Nairobi
São Paulo Shanghai Taipei Tokyo Toronto

Oxford is a registered trade mark of Oxford University Press
in the UK and in certain other countries

© Selection, Notes, and Approaches:
Dr Peter Mack and Chris Walton 1995
Poem text: Larry D. Benson (Editor), *The Riverside Chaucer*,
Third Edition. Copyright © 1987 by Houghton Mifflin Company.
Reprinted with permission.

ISBN 0 19 831988 6

Other titles in the series

Typeset by Pentacor PLC, High Wycombe, Bucks
Printed and bound in Great Britain by Alden Press Ltd, Oxford
The publishers would like to thank the following for permission to reproduce
photographs: The Mansell Collection p. 141; Museum of the History of Science, Oxford University
p. 142; The British Library p. 144. The illustration on p. 143 is by Jason Lewis.
The cover illustration is by John Rushton.

Contents

Acknowledgements

Peter Mack would like to acknowledge the help he received in compiling the Notes from the critical works and editions listed in Further Reading, and from his colleagues, Gloria Cigman and Bill Whitehead. He is grateful to Robert Burchfield for his comments on the Note on Chaucer's English. Chris Walton would like to thank his A-level students for their comments on the Approaches, Erica Holley for valuable historical resources, and Barbara Mitchell for providing critical material. Both editors would like to thank Victor Lee and Lucy Hooper, for their constructive criticism and advice. The text is taken from L. D. Benson ed., *The Riverside Chaucer* (Cambridge, Mass, 1987), with permission.

Editors

Dr Victor Lee, the series editor, read English at University College, Cardiff. He was later awarded his doctorate at the University of Oxford. He has taught at secondary and tertiary level, and is currently working at the Open University. Victor Lee's experience as an examiner is very wide: he has been a Chief Examiner in English A-level for three different boards stretching over a period of twenty years.

Dr Peter Mack read English at St Peter's College, Oxford and went on to gain an MPhil and PhD in Renaissance Studies from The Warburg Institute, University of London. He has examined English at 0 and A-level as well as for the International Baccalaureate. He is now a Senior Lecturer in the Department of English at Warwick University where he has taught Medieval English Studies since 1979. His other books include: *Renaissance Argument* (1993) and *Renaissance Rhetoric* (1994).

Chris Walton read English Literature and Philosophy at Leeds University. He teaches English at The Ridgeway School in Wiltshire, where he has developed a modular A-level English syllabus. He recently gained an MPhil in classroom research at Bath University. He has also written GCSE and A-level examination revision guides.

Foreword

Oxford Student Texts are specifically aimed at presenting poetry and drama to an audience which is studying English Literature at an advanced level. Each text is designed as an integrated whole consisting of three main parts. The poetry or the play is always placed first to stress its importance and to encourage students to enjoy it without secondary critical material of any kind. When help is needed on other occasions, the second and third parts of these texts, the Notes and the Approaches provide it.

The Notes perform two functions. First, they provide information and explain allusions. Secondly, and this is where they differ from most texts at this level, they often raise questions of central concern to the interpretation of the poem or the play being dealt with, particularly in the use of a general note placed at the beginning of the particular notes.

The third part, the Approaches section, deals with major issues of response to the particular selection of poetry or drama, as opposed to the work of the writer as a whole. One of the major aims of this part of the text is to emphasize that there is no one right answer to interpretation, but a series of approaches. Readers are given guidance as to what counts as evidence, but, in the end, left to make up their mind as to which are the most suitable interpretations, or to add their own.

To help achieve this, the Approaches section contains a number of activity-discussion sequences, although it must be stressed that these are optional. Significant issues about the poetry or the play are raised in these activities. Readers are invited to tackle these activities before proceeding to the discussion section where possible reponses to the questions raised in the activities are considered. Their main function is to engage readers actively in the ideas of the text. However, these activity-discussion sequences are so arranged that, if readers wish to treat the Approaches as continuous prose and not attempt the activities, they can.

At the end of each text there is also a list of Tasks. Whereas the activity-discussion sequences are aimed at increasing understanding of the literary work itself, these tasks are intended to help explore ideas about the poetry or the play after the student has completed the reading of the work and the studying of the Notes and Approaches. These tasks are particularly helpful for coursework projects or in preparing for an examination.

Victor Lee   Series Editor

The Miller's Tale

The Miller's Portrait: General Prologue

545   The MILLERE was a stout carl for the nones;
Ful byg he was of brawn, and eek of bones.
That proved wel, for over al ther he cam,
At wrastlynge he wolde have alwey the ram.
He was short-sholdred, brood, a thikke knarre;
550   Ther was no dore that he nolde heve of harre,
Or breke it at a rennyng with his heed.
His berd as any sowe or fox was reed,
And therto brood, as though it were a spade.
Upon the cop right of his nose he hade
555   A werte, and theron stood a toft of herys,
Reed as the brustles of a sowes erys;
His nosethirles blake were and wyde.
A swerd and a bokeler bar he by his syde.
His mouth as greet was as a greet forneys.
560   He was a janglere and a goliardeys,
And that was moost of synne and harlotries.
Wel koude he stelen corn and tollen thries;
And yet he hadde a thombe of gold, pardee.
A whit cote and a blew hood wered he.
565   A baggepipe wel koude he blowe and sowne,
And therwithal he broghte us out of towne.

The Miller's Prologue

Heere folwen the wordes bitwene the Hoost and the Millere.

    Whan that the Knyght had thus his tale ytoold,
In al the route nas ther yong ne oold
That he ne seyde it was a noble storie
And worthy for to drawen to memorie,
5 And namely the gentils everichon.
Oure Hooste lough and swoor, 'So moot I gon,
This gooth aright; unbokeled is the male.
Lat se now who shal telle another tale;
For trewely the game is wel bigonne.
10 Now telleth ye, sir Monk, if that ye konne,
Somwhat to quite with the Knyghtes tale.'
The Millere, that for dronken was al pale,
So that unnethe upon his hors he sat,
He nolde avalen neither hood ne hat,
15 Ne abyde no man for his curteisie,
But in Pilates voys he gan to crie,
And swoor, 'By armes, and by blood and bones,
I kan a noble tale for the nones,
With which I wol now quite the Knyghtes tale.'
20 Oure Hooste saugh that he was dronke of ale,
And seyde, 'Abyd, Robyn, my leeve brother;
Som bettre man shal telle us first another.
Abyd, and lat us werken thriftily.'
    'By Goddes soule,' quod he, 'that wol nat I;
25 For I wol speke or elles go my wey.'
Oure Hoost answerde, 'Tel on, a devel wey!
Thou art a fool; thy wit is overcome.'
    'Now herkneth,' quod the Millere, 'alle and some!
But first I make a protestacioun

30   That I am dronke; I knowe it by my soun.
And therfore if that I mysspeke or seye,
Wyte it the ale of Southwerk, I you preye.
For I wol telle a legende and a lyf
Bothe of a carpenter and of his wyf,

35   How that a clerk hath set the wrightes cappe.'
     The Reve answerde and seyde, 'Stynt thy clappe!
Lat be thy lewed dronken harlotrye.
It is a synne and eek a greet folye
To apeyren any man, or hym defame,

40   And eek to bryngen wyves in swich fame.
Thou mayst ynogh of othere thynges seyn.'
     This dronke Millere spak ful soone ageyn
And seyde, 'Leve brother Osewold,
Who hath no wyf, he is no cokewold.

45   But I sey nat therfore that thou art oon;
Ther been ful goode wyves many oon,
And evere a thousand goode ayeyns oon badde.
That knowestow wel thyself, but if thou madde.
Why artow angry with my tale now?

50   I have a wyf, pardee, as wel as thow;
Yet nolde I, for the oxen in my plogh,
Take upon me moore than ynogh,
As demen of myself that I were oon;
I wol bileve wel that I am noon.

55   An housbonde shal nat been inquisityf
Of Goddes pryvetee, nor of his wyf.
So he may fynde Goddes foyson there,
Of the remenant nedeth nat enquere.'
     What sholde I moore seyn, but this Millere

60   He nolde his wordes for no man forbere,
But tolde his cherles tale in his manere.
M'athynketh that I shal reherce it heere.
And therfore every gentil wight I preye,

For Goddes love, demeth nat that I seye
65   Of yvel entente, but for I moot reherce
Hir tales alle, be they bettre or werse,
Or elles falsen som of my mateere.
And therfore, whoso list it nat yheere,
Turne over the leef and chese another tale;
70   For he shal fynde ynowe, grete and smale,
Of storial thyng that toucheth gentillesse,
And eek moralitee and hoolynesse.
Blameth nat me if that ye chese amys.
The Millere is a cherl; ye knowe wel this.
75   So was the Reve eek and othere mo,
And harlotrie they tolden bothe two.
Avyseth yow, and put me out of blame;
And eek men shal nat maken ernest of game.

The Miller's Tale

Heere bigynneth the Millere his tale.

Whilom ther was dwellynge at Oxenford
80   A riche gnof, that gestes heeld to bord,
And of his craft he was a carpenter.
With hym ther was dwellynge a poure scoler,
Hadde lerned art, but al his fantasye
Was turned for to lerne astrologye,
85   And koude a certeyn of conclusiouns,
To demen by interrogaciouns,
If that men asked hym, in certein houres
Whan that men sholde have droghte or elles shoures,
Or if men asked hym what sholde bifalle
90   Of every thyng; I may nat rekene hem alle.

This clerk was cleped hende Nicholas.
Of deerne love he koude and of solas;
And therto he was sleigh and ful privee,
And lyk a mayden meke for to see.
95   A chambre hadde he in that hostelrye
Allone, withouten any compaignye,
Ful fetisly ydight with herbes swoote;
And he hymself as sweete as is the roote
Of lycorys or any cetewale.
100 His Almageste, and bookes grete and smale,
His astrelabie, longynge for his art,
His augrym stones layen faire apart,
On shelves couched at his beddes heed;
His presse ycovered with a faldyng reed;
105 And al above ther lay a gay sautrie,
On which he made a-nyghtes melodie
So swetely that all the chambre rong;
And *Angelus ad virginem* he song;
And after that he song the Kynges Noote.
110 Ful often blessed was his myrie throte.
And thus this sweete clerk his tyme spente
After his freendes fyndyng and his rente.
    This carpenter hadde wedded newe a wyf,
Which that he lovede moore than his lyf;
115 Of eighteteene yeer she was of age.
Jalous he was, and heeld hire narwe in cage,
For she was wylde and yong, and he was old
And demed hymself been lik a cokewold.
He knew nat Catoun, for his wit was rude,
120 That bad man sholde wedde his simylitude.
Men sholde wedden after hire estaat,
For youthe and elde is often at debaat.
But sith that he was fallen in the snare,
He moste endure, as oother folk, his care.

125   Fair was this yonge wyf, and therwithal
       As any wezele hir body gent and smal.
       A ceynt she werede, barred al of silk,
       A barmclooth as whit as morne milk
       Upon hir lendes, ful of many a goore.
130   Whit was hir smok, and broyden al bifoore
       And eek bihynde, on hir coler aboute,
       Of col-blak silk, withinne and eek withoute.
       The tapes of hir white voluper
       Were of the same suyte of hir coler;
135   Hir filet brood of silk, and set ful hye.
       And sikerly she hadde a likerous ye;
       Ful smale ypulled were hire browes two,
       And tho were bent and blake as any sloo.
       She was ful moore blisful on to see
140   Than is the newe pere-jonette tree,
       And softer than the wolle is of a wether.
       And by hir girdel heeng a purs of lether,
       Tasseled with silk and perled with latoun.
       In al this world, to seken up and doun,
145   There nys no man so wys that koude thenche
       So gay a popelote or swich a wenche.
       Ful brighter was the shynyng of hir hewe
       Than in the Tour the noble yforged newe.
       But of hir song, it was as loude and yerne
150   As any swalwe sittynge on a berne.
       Therto she koude skippe and make game,
       As any kyde or calf folwynge his dame.
       Hir mouth was sweete as bragot or the meeth,
       Or hoord of apples leyd in hey or heeth.
155   Wynsynge she was, as is a joly colt,
       Long as a mast, and upright as a bolt.
       A brooch she baar upon hir lowe coler,
       As brood as is the boos of a bokeler.

Hir shoes were laced on hir legges hye.
160 She was a prymerole, a piggesnye,
     For any lord to leggen in his bedde,
     Or yet for any good yeman to wedde.
          Now, sire, and eft, sire, so bifel the cas
     That on a day this hende Nicholas
165 Fil with this yonge wyf to rage and pleye,
     Whil that hir housbonde was at Oseneye,
     As clerkes ben ful subtile and ful queynte;
     And prively he caughte hire by the queynte,
     And seyde, 'Ywis, but if ich have my wille,
170 For deerne love of thee, lemman, I spille.'
     And heeld hire harde by the haunchebones,
     And seyde, 'Lemman, love me al atones,
     Or I wol dyen, also God me save!'
     And she sproong as a colt dooth in the trave,
175 And with hir heed she wryed faste awey,
     And seyde, 'I wol nat kisse thee, by my fey!
     Why, lat be!' quod she. 'Lat be, Nicholas,
     Or I wol crie "out, harrow" and "allas"!
     Do wey youre handes, for youre curteisye!'
180   This Nicholas gan mercy for to crye,
     And spak so faire, and profred him so faste,
     That she hir love hym graunted atte laste,
     And swoor hir ooth, by Seint Thomas of Kent,
     That she wol been at his comandement,
185 Whan that she may hir leyser wel espie.
     'Myn housbonde is so ful of jalousie
     That but ye wayte wel and been privee,
     I woot right wel I nam but deed,' quod she.
     'Ye moste been ful deerne, as in this cas.'
190   'Nay, therof care thee noght,' quod Nicholas.
     'A clerk hadde litherly biset his whyle,
     But if he koude a carpenter bigyle.'

And thus they been accorded and ysworn
To wayte a tyme, as I have told biforn.
195   Whan Nicholas had doon thus everideel
And thakked hire aboute the lendes weel,
He kiste hire sweete and taketh his sawtrie,
And pleyeth faste, and maketh melodie.
        Thanne fil it thus, that to the paryssh chirche,
200   Cristes owene werkes for to wirche,
This goode wyf went on an haliday.
Hir forheed shoon as bright as any day,
So was it wasshen whan she leet hir werk.
Now was ther of that chirche a parissh clerk,
205   The which that was ycleped Absolon.
Crul was his heer, and as the gold it shoon,
And strouted as a fanne large and brode;
Ful streight and evene lay his joly shode.
His rode was reed, his eyen greye as goos.
210   With Poules wyndow corven on his shoos,
In hoses rede he wente fetisly.
Yclad he was ful smal and proprely
Al in a kirtel of a lyght waget;
Ful faire and thikke been the poyntes set.
215   And therupon he hadde a gay surplys
As whit as is the blosme upon the rys.
A myrie child he was, so God me save.
Wel koude he laten blood, and clippe and shave,
And maken a chartre of lond or acquitaunce.
220   In twenty manere koude he trippe and daunce
After the scole of Oxenforde tho,
And with his legges casten to and fro,
And pleyen songes on a smal rubible;
Therto he song som tyme a loud quynyble;
225   And as wel koude he pleye on a giterne.
In al the toun nas brewhous ne taverne

That he ne visited with his solas,
Ther any gaylard tappestere was.
But sooth to seyn, he was somdeel squaymous
230 Of fartyng, and of speche daungerous.
    This Absolon, that jolif was and gay,
Gooth with a sencer on the haliday,
Sensynge the wyves of the parisshe faste;
And many a lovely look on hem he caste,
235 And namely on this carpenteris wyf.
To looke on hire hym thoughte a myrie lyf,
She was so propre and sweete and likerous.
I dar wel seyn, if she hadde been a mous,
And he a cat, he wolde hire hente anon.
240 This parissh clerk, this joly Absolon,
Hath in his herte swich a love-longynge
That of no wyf took he noon offrynge;
For curteisie, he seyde, he wolde noon.
    The moone, whan it was nyght, ful brighte shoon,
245 And Absolon his gyterne hath ytake;
For paramours he thoghte for to wake.
And forth he gooth, jolif and amorous,
Til he cam to the carpenteres hous
A litel after cokkes hadde ycrowe,
250 And dressed hym up by a shot-wyndowe
That was upon the carpenteris wal.
He syngeth in his voys gentil and smal,
'Now, deere lady, if thy wille be,
I praye yow that ye wole rewe on me,'
255 Ful wel acordaunt to his gyternynge.
This carpenter awook, and herde him synge,
And spak unto his wyf, and seyde anon,
'What! Alison! Herestow nat Absolon,
That chaunteth thus under oure boures wal?'
260 And she answerde hir housbonde therwithal,

'Yis, God woot, John, I heere it every deel.'
This passeth forth; what wol ye bet than weel?
Fro day to day this joly Absolon
So woweth hire that hym is wo bigon.
265 He waketh al the nyght and al the day;
He kembeth his lokkes brode, and made hym gay;
He woweth hire by meenes and brocage,
And swoor he wolde been hir owene page;
He syngeth, brokkynge as a nyghtyngale;
270 He sente hire pyment, meeth, and spiced ale,
And wafres, pipyng hoot out of the gleede;
And, for she was of town, he profred meede;
For som folk wol ben wonnen for richesse,
And somme for strokes, and somme for gentillesse.
275 Somtyme, to shewe his lightnesse and maistrye,
He pleyeth Herodes upon a scaffold hye.
But what availleth hym as in this cas?
She loveth so this hende Nicholas
That Absolon may blowe the bukkes horn;
280 He ne hadde for his labour but a scorn.
And thus she maketh Absolon hire ape,
And al his ernest turneth til a jape.
Ful sooth is this proverbe, it is no lye,
Men seyn right thus: 'Alwey the nye slye
285 Maketh the ferre leeve to be looth.'
For though that Absolon be wood or wrooth,
By cause that he fer was from hire sight,
This nye Nicholas stood in his light.
Now ber thee wel, thou hende Nicholas,
290 For Absolon may waille and synge 'allas.'
And so bifel it on a Saterday,
This carpenter was goon til Osenay;
And hende Nicholas and Alisoun
Acorded been to this conclusioun,

295 That Nicholas shal shapen hym a wyle
     This sely jalous housbonde to bigyle;
     And if so be the game wente aright,
     She sholde slepen in his arm al nyght,
     For this was his desir and hire also.
300 And right anon, withouten wordes mo,
     This Nicholas no lenger wolde tarie,
     But dooth ful softe unto his chambre carie
     Bothe mete and drynke for a day or tweye,
     And to hire housbonde bad hire for to seye,
305 If that he axed after Nicholas,
     She sholde seye she nyste where he was;
     Of al that day she saugh hym nat with ye;
     She trowed that he was in maladye,
     For, for no cry hir mayde koude hym calle,
310 He nolde answere for thyng that myghte falle.
         This passeth forth al thilke Saterday,
     That Nicholas stille in his chambre lay,
     And eet and sleep, or dide what hym leste,
     Til Sonday, that the sonne gooth to reste.
315 This sely carpenter hath greet merveyle
     Of Nicholas, or what thyng myghte hym eyle,
     And seyde, 'I am adrad, by Seint Thomas,
     It stondeth nat aright with Nicholas.
     God shilde that he deyde sodeynly!
320 This world is now ful tikel, sikerly.
     I saugh today a cors yborn to chirche
     That now, on Monday last, I saugh hym wirche.
         'Go up,' quod he unto his knave anoon,
     'Clepe at his dore, or knokke with a stoon.
325 Looke how it is, and tel me boldely.'
         This knave gooth hym up ful sturdily,
     And at the chambre dore whil that he stood,
     He cride and knokked as that he were wood,

'What, how! What do ye, maister Nicholay?
330   How may ye slepen al the longe day?'
      But al for noght; he herde nat a word.
An hole he foond, ful lowe upon a bord,
Ther as the cat was wont in for to crepe,
And at that hole he looked in ful depe,
335   And at the laste he hadde of hym a sight.
This Nicholas sat evere capyng upright,
As he had kiked on the newe moone.
Adoun he gooth, and tolde his maister soone
In what array he saugh this ilke man.
340   This carpenter to blessen hym bigan,
And seyde, 'Help us, Seinte Frydeswyde!
A man woot litel what hym shal bityde.
This man is falle, with his astromye,
In some woodnesse or in som agonye.
345   I thoghte ay wel how that it sholde be!
Men sholde nat knowe of Goddes pryvetee.
Ye, blessed be alwey a lewed man
That noght but oonly his bileve kan!
So ferde another clerk with astromye;
350   He walked in the feeldes for to prye
Upon the sterres, what ther sholde bifalle,
Til he was in a marle-pit yfalle;
He saugh nat that. But yet, by Seint Thomas,
Me reweth soore of hende Nicholas.
355   He shal be rated of his studiyng,
If that I may, by Jhesus, hevene kyng!
Get me a staf, that I may underspore,
Whil that thou, Robyn, hevest up the dore.
He shal out of his studiyng, as I gesse.'
360   And to the chambre dore he gan hym dresse.
His knave was a strong carl for the nones,
And by the haspe he haaf it of atones;

Into the floor the dore fil anon.
This Nicholas sat ay as stille as stoon,
365 And evere caped upward into the eir.
This carpenter wende he were in despeir,
And hente hym by the sholdres myghtily,
And shook hym harde, and cride spitously,
'What! Nicholay! What, how! What, looke adoun!
370 Awak, and thenk on Cristes passioun!
I crouche thee from elves and fro wightes.'
Therwith the nyght-spel seyde he anon-rightes
On foure halves of the hous aboute,
And on the thresshfold of the dore withoute:
375 'Jhesu Crist and Seinte Benedight,
Blesse this hous from every wikked wight,
For nyghtes verye, the white *pater-noster!*
Where wentestow, Seinte Petres soster?'
And atte laste this hende Nicholas
380 Gan for to sik soore, and seyde, 'Allas!
Shal al the world be lost eftsoones now?'
This carpenter answerde, 'What seystow?
What! Thynk on God, as we doon, men that swynke.'
This Nicholas answerde, 'Fecche me drynke,
385 And after wol I speke in pryvetee
Of certeyn thyng that toucheth me and thee.
I wol telle it noon oother man, certeyn.'
This carpenter goth doun, and comth ageyn,
And broghte of myghty ale a large quart;
390 And whan that ech of hem had dronke his part,
This Nicholas his dore faste shette,
And doun the carpenter by hym he sette.
He seyde 'John, myn hooste, lief and deere,
Thou shalt upon thy trouthe swere me heere
395 That to no wight thou shalt this conseil wreye,
For it is Cristes conseil that I seye,

And if thou telle it man, thou art forlore;
For this vengeaunce thou shalt han therfore,
That if thou wreye me, thou shalt be wood.'
400 'Nay, Crist forbede it, for his hooly blood!'
Quod tho this sely man, 'I nam no labbe,
Ne, though I seye, I nam nat lief to gabbe.
Sey what thou wolt, I shal it nevere telle
To child ne wyf, by hym that harwed helle!'
405   'Now John,' quod Nicholas, 'I wol nat lye;
I have yfounde in myn astrologye,
As I have looked in the moone bright,
That now a Monday next, at quarter nyght,
Shal falle a reyn, and that so wilde and wood
410 That half so greet was nevere Noes flood.
This world,' he seyde, 'in lasse than an hour
Shal al be dreynt, so hidous is the shour.
Thus shal mankynde drenche, and lese hir lyf.'
    This carpenter answerde, 'Allas, my wyf!
415 And shal she drenche? Allas, myn Alisoun!'
For sorwe of this he fil almoost adoun,
And seyde, 'Is ther no remedie in this cas?'
    'Why, yis, for Gode,' quod hende Nicholas,
'If thou wolt werken after loore and reed.
420 Thou mayst nat werken after thyn owene heed;
For thus seith Salomon, that was ful trewe:
"Werk al by conseil, and thou shalt nat rewe."
And if thou werken wolt by good conseil,
I undertake, withouten mast and seyl,
425 Yet shal I saven hire and thee and me.
Hastow nat herd hou saved was Noe,
Whan that oure Lord hadde warned hym biforn
That al the world with water sholde be lorn?'
    'Yis,' quod this Carpenter, 'ful yoore ago.'
430   'Hastou nat herd,' quod Nicholas, 'also

14

The sorwe of Noe with his felaweshipe,
Er that he myghte gete his wyf to shipe?
Hym hadde be levere, I dar wel undertake,
At thilke tyme, than alle his wetheres blake

435 That she hadde had a ship hirself allone.
And therfore, woostou what is best to doone?
This asketh haste, and of an hastif thyng
Men may nat preche or maken tariyng.

'Anon go gete us faste into this in

440 A knedyng trogh, or ellis a kymelyn,
For ech of us, but looke that they be large,
In which we mowe swymme as in a barge,
And han therinne vitaille suffisant
But for a day – fy on the remenant!

445 The water shal aslake and goon away
Aboute pryme upon the nexte day.
But Robyn may nat wite of this, thy knave,
Ne eek thy mayde Gille I may nat save;
Axe nat why, for though thou aske me,

450 I wol nat tellen Goddes pryvetee.
Suffiseth thee, but if thy wittes madde,
To han as greet a grace as Noe hadde.
Thy wyf shal I wel saven, out of doute.
Go now thy wey, and speed thee heer-aboute.

455 'But whan thou hast, for hire and thee and me,
Ygeten us thise knedyng tubbes thre,
Thanne shaltow hange hem in the roof ful hye,
That no man of oure purveiaunce espye.
And whan thou thus hast doon as I have seyd,

460 And hast oure vitaille faire in hem yleyd,
And eek an ax to smyte the corde atwo,
Whan that the water comth, that we may go
And breke an hole an heigh, upon the gable,
Unto the gardyn-ward, over the stable,

465 That we may frely passen forth oure way,
   Whan that the grete shour is goon away.
   Thanne shaltou swymme as myrie, I undertake,
   As dooth the white doke after hire drake.
   Thanne wol I clepe, "How, Alison! How, John!
470 Be myrie, for the flood wol passe anon."
   And thou wolt seyn, "Hayl, maister Nicholay!
   Good morwe, I se thee wel, for it is day."
   And thanne shul we be lordes al oure lyf
   Of al the world, as Noe and his wyf.
475   'But of o thyng I warne thee ful right:
   Be wel avysed on that ilke nyght
   That we ben entred into shippes bord,
   That noon of us ne speke nat a word,
   Ne clepe, ne crie, but be in his preyere;
480 For it is Goddes owene heeste deere.
       'Thy wyf and thou moote hange fer atwynne;
   For that bitwixe yow shal be no synne,
   Namoore in lookyng than ther shal in deede.
   This ordinance is seyd. Go, God thee speede!
485 Tomorwe at nyght, whan men ben alle aslepe,
   Into oure knedyng-tubbes wol we crepe,
   And sitten there, abidyng Goddes grace.
   Go now thy wey; I have no lenger space
   To make of this no lenger sermonyng.
490 Men seyn thus, "sende the wise, and sey no thyng."
   Thou art so wys, it needeth thee nat teche.
   Go, save oure lyf, and that I the biseche.'
       This sely carpenter goth forth his wey.
   Ful ofte he seide 'Allas and weylawey,'
495 And to his wyf he tolde his pryvetee,
   And she was war, and knew it bet than he,
   What al this queynte cast was for to seye.
   But nathelees she ferde as she wolde deye,

And seyde, 'Allas! go forth thy wey anon,
500 Help us to scape, or we been dede echon!
I am thy trewe, verray wedded wyf;
Go, deere spouse, and help to save oure lyf.'
    Lo, which a greet thyng is affeccioun!
Men may dyen of ymaginacioun,
505 So depe may impressioun be take.
This sely carpenter bigynneth quake;
Hym thynketh verraily that he may see
Noees flood come walwynge as the see
To drenchen Alisoun, his hony deere.
510 He wepeth, weyleth, maketh sory cheere;
He siketh with ful many a sory swogh;
He gooth and geteth hym a knedyng trogh,
And after that a tubbe and a kymelyn,
And pryvely he sente hem to his in,
515 And heng hem in the roof in pryvetee.
His owene hand he made laddres thre,
To clymben by the ronges and the stalkes
Unto the tubbes hangynge in the balkes,
And hem vitailled, bothe trogh and tubbe,
520 With breed, and chese, and good ale in a jubbe,
Suffisynge right ynogh as for a day.
But er that he hadde maad al this array,
He sente his knave, and eek his wenche also,
Upon his nede to London for to go.
525 And on the Monday, whan it drow to nyght,
He shette his dore withoute candel-lyght,
And dressed alle thyng as it sholde be.
And shortly, up they clomben alle thre;
They seten stille wel a furlong way.
530   'Now, *Pater-noster*, clom!' seyde Nicholay,
And 'Clom!' quod John, and 'Clom!' seyde Alisoun.
This carpenter seyde his devocioun,

And stille he sit, and biddeth his preyere,
Awaitynge on the reyn, if he it heere.

535   The dede sleep, for wery bisynesse,
Fil on this carpenter right, as I gesse,
Aboute corfew-tyme, or litel moore;
For travaille of his goost he groneth soore,
And eft he routeth, for his heed myslay.

540   Doun of the laddre stalketh Nicholay,
And Alisoun ful softe adoun she spedde;
Withouten wordes mo they goon to bedde,
Ther as the carpenter is wont to lye.
Ther was the revel and the melodye;

545   And thus lith Alison and Nicholas,
In bisynesse of myrthe and of solas,
Til that the belle of laudes gan to rynge,
And freres in the chauncel gonne synge.
    This parissh clerk, this amorous Absolon,

550   That is for love alwey so wo bigon,
Upon the Monday was at Oseneye
With compaignye, hym to disporte and pleye,
And axed upon cas a cloisterer
Ful prively after John the carpenter;

555   And he drough hym apart out of the chirche,
And seyde, 'I noot; I saugh hym heere nat wirche
Syn Saterday; I trowe that he be went
For tymber, ther oure abbot hath hym sent;
For he is wont for tymber for to go

560   And dwellen at the grange a day or two;
Or elles he is at his hous, certeyn.
Where that he be, I kan nat soothly seyn.'
    This Absolon ful joly was and light,
And thoghte, 'Now is tyme to wake al nyght,

565   For sikirly I saugh hym nat stirynge
Aboute his dore, syn day bigan to sprynge.

'So moot I thryve, I shal, at cokkes crowe,
Ful pryvely knokken at his wyndowe
That stant ful lowe upon his boures wal.
570 To Alison now wol I tellen al
My love-longynge, for yet I shal nat mysse
That at the leeste wey I shal hire kisse.
Som maner confort shal I have, parfay.
My mouth hath icched al this longe day;
575 That is a signe of kissyng atte leeste.
Al nyght me mette eek I was at a feeste.
Therfore I wol go slepe an houre or tweye,
And al the nyght thanne wol I wake and pleye.'
Whan that the firste cok hath crowe, anon
580 Up rist this joly lovere Absolon,
And hym arraieth gay, at poynt-devys.
But first he cheweth greyn and lycorys,
To smellen sweete, er he hadde kembd his heer.
Under his tonge a trewe-love he beer,
585 For therby wende he to ben gracious.
He rometh to the carpenteres hous,
And stille he stant under the shot-wyndowe —
Unto his brest it raughte, it was so lowe —
And softe he cougheth with a semy soun:
590 'What do ye, hony-comb, sweete Alisoun,
My faire bryd, my sweete cynamome?
Awaketh, lemman myn, and speketh to me!
Wel litel thynken ye upon my wo,
That for youre love I swete ther I go.
595 No wonder is thogh that I swelte and swete;
I moorne as dooth a lamb after the tete.
Ywis, lemman, I have swich love-longynge
That lik a turtel trewe is my moornynge.
I may nat ete na moore than a mayde.'
600 'Go fro the wyndow, Jakke fool,' she sayde;

'As help me God, it wol nat be "com pa me."
I love another – and elles I were to blame —
Wel bet than thee, by Jhesu, Absolon.
Go forth thy wey, or I wol caste a ston,
605   And lat me slepe, a twenty devel wey!'
    'Allas,' quod Absolon, 'and weylawey,
That trewe love was evere so yvel biset!
Thanne kysse me, syn it may be no bet,
For Jhesus love, and for the love of me.'
610   'Wiltow thanne go thy wey therwith?' quod she.
    'Ye, certes, lemman,' quod this Absolon.
    'Thanne make thee redy,' quod she, 'I come anon.'
And unto Nicholas she seyde stille,
'Now hust, and thou shalt laughen al thy fille.'
615   This Absolon doun sette hym on his knees
And seyde, 'I am a lord at alle degrees;
For after this I hope ther cometh moore.
Lemman, thy grace, and sweete bryd, thyn oore!'
    The wyndow she undoth, and that in haste.
620 'Have do,' quod she, 'com of, and speed the faste,
Lest that oure neighebores thee espie.'
    This Absolon gan wype his mouth ful drie.
Derk was the nyght as pich, or as the cole,
And at the wyndow out she putte hir hole,
625 And Absolon, hym fil no bet ne wers,
But with his mouth he kiste hir naked ers
Ful savourly, er he were war of this.
Abak he stirte, and thoughte it was amys,
For wel he wiste a womman hath no berd.
630 He felte a thyng al rough and long yherd,
And seyde, 'Fy! allas! what have I do?'
    'Tehee!' quod she, and clapte the wyndow to,
And Absolon gooth forth a sory pas.
    'A berd! A berd!' quod hende Nicholas,

635 'By Goddes corpus, this goth faire and weel.'
 This sely Absolon herde every deel,
And on his lippe he gan for anger byte,
And to hymself he seyde, 'I shal thee quyte.'
 Who rubbeth now, who froteth now his lippes
640 With dust, with sond, with straw, with clooth, with
  chippes,
But Absolon, that seith ful ofte, 'Allas!'
'My soule bitake I unto Sathanas,
But me were levere than al this toun,' quod he,
'Of this despit awroken for to be.
645 Allas,' quod he, 'allas, I ne hadde ybleynt!'
His hoote love was coold and al yqueynt;
For fro that tyme that he hadde kist hir ers,
Of paramours he sette nat a kers,
For he was heeled of his maladie.
650 Ful ofte paramours he gan deffie,
And weep as dooth a child that is ybete.
A softe paas he wente over the strete
Until a smyth men cleped daun Gerveys,
That in his forge smythed plough harneys;
655 He sharpeth shaar and kultour bisily.
This Absolon knokketh al esily,
And seyde, 'Undo, Gerveys, and that anon.'
 'What, who artow?' 'It am I, Absolon.'
'What, Absolon! for Cristes sweete tree,
660 Why rise ye so rathe? Ey, benedicitee!
What eyleth yow? Som gay gerl, God it woot,
Hath broght yow thus upon the viritoot.
By Seinte Note, ye woot wel what I mene.'
 This Absolon ne roghte nat a bene
665 Of al his pley; no word agayn he yaf;
He hadde moore tow on his distaf
Than Gerveys knew, and seyde, 'Freend so deere,

That hoote kultour in the chymenee heere,
As lene it me; I have therwith to doone,
670 And I wol brynge it thee agayn ful soone.'
    Gerveys answerde, 'Certes, were it gold,
Or in a poke nobles alle untold,
Thou sholdest have, as I am trewe smyth.
Ey, Cristes foo! What wol ye do therwith?'
675 'Therof,' quod Absolon, 'be as be may.
I shal wel telle it thee to-morwe day' —
And caughte the kultour by the colde stele.
Ful softe out at the dore he gan to stele,
And wente unto the carpenteris wal.
680 He cogheth first, and knokketh therwithal
Upon the wyndowe, right as he dide er.
    This Alison answerde, 'Who is ther
That knokketh so? I warante it a theef.'
    'Why, nay,' quod he, 'God woot, my sweete leef,
685 I am thyn Absolon, my deerelyng.
Of gold,' quod he, 'I have thee broght a ryng.
My mooder yaf it me, so God me save;
Ful fyn it is, and therto wel ygrave.
This wol I yeve thee, if thou me kisse.'
690   This Nicholas was risen for to pisse,
And thoughte he wolde amenden al the jape;
He sholde kisse his ers er that he scape.
And up the wyndowe dide he hastily,
And out his ers he putteth pryvely
695 Over the buttok, to the haunche-bon;
And therwith spak this clerk, this Absolon,
'Spek, sweete bryd, I noot nat where thou art.'
    This Nicholas anon leet fle a fart
As greet as it had been a thonder-dent,
700 That with the strook he was almoost yblent;
And he was redy with his iren hoot,

And Nicholas amydde the ers he smoot.
   Of gooth the skyn an hande-brede aboute,
The hoote kultour brende so his toute,
705 And for the smert he wende for to dye.
As he were wood, for wo he gan to crye,
'Help! Water! Water! Help, for Goddes herte!'
   This carpenter out of his slomber sterte,
And herde oon crien 'water!' as he were wood,
710 And thoughte, 'Allas, now comth Nowelis flood!'
He sit hym up withouten wordes mo,
And with his ax he smoot the corde atwo,
And doun gooth al; he foond neither to selle,
Ne breed ne ale, til he cam to the celle
715 Upon the floor, and ther aswowne he lay.
   Up stirte hire Alison and Nicholay,
And criden 'Out' and 'Harrow' in the strete.
The neighebores, bothe smale and grete,
In ronnen for to gauren on this man,
720 That yet aswowne lay, bothe pale and wan,
For with the fal he brosten hadde his arm.
But stonde he moste unto his owene harm;
For whan he spak, he was anon bore doun
With hende Nicholas and Alisoun.
725 They tolden every man that he was wood;
He was agast so of Nowelis flood
Thurgh fantasie that of his vanytee
He hadde yboght hym knedyng tubbes thre,
And hadde hem hanged in the roof above;
730 And that he preyed hem, for Goddes love,
To sitten in the roof, *par compaignye*.
   The folk gan laughen at his fantasye;
Into the roof they kiken and they cape,
And turned al his harm unto a jape.
735 For what so that this carpenter answerde,

It was for noght; no man his reson herde.
With othes grete he was so sworn adoun
That he was holde wood in al the toun;
For every clerk anonright heeld with oother.
740 They seyde, 'The man is wood, my leeve brother';
And every wight gan laughen at this stryf.
Thus swyved was this carpenteris wyf,
For al his kepyng and his jalousye,
And Absolon hath kist hir nether ye,
745 And Nicholas is scalded in the towte.
This tale is doon, and God save al the rowte!

Heere endeth the Millere his tale.

The Reeve's Prologue

The prologe of the Reves Tale.

Whan folk hadde laughen at this nyce cas
Of Absolon and hende Nicholas,
Diverse folk diversely they seyde,
750 But for the moore part they loughe and pleyde.
Ne at this tale I saugh no man hym greve,
But it were oonly Osewold the Reve.
By cause he was of carpenteris craft,
A litel ire is in his herte ylaft;
755 He gan to grucche, and blamed it a lite.
'So theek,' quod he, 'ful wel koude I thee quite
With bleryng of a proud milleres ye,
If that me liste speke of ribaudye.
But ik am oold; me list not pley for age;
760 Gras tyme is doon; my fodder is now forage;
This white top writeth myne olde yeris,

Myn herte is also mowled as myne heris,
But if I fare as dooth an open-ers —
That ilke fruyt is ever lenger the wers,
765 Til it be roten in mullok or in stree.
We olde men, I drede, so fare we:
Til we be roten, kan we nat be rype;
We hoppen alwey whil that the world wol pype.
For in oure wyl ther stiketh evere a nayl,
770 To have an hoor heed and a grene tayl,
As hath a leek; for thogh oure myght be goon,
Oure wyl desireth folie evere in oon.
For whan we may nat doon, than wol we speke;
Yet in oure asshen olde is fyr yreke.
775   'Foure gleedes han we, which I shal devyse —
Avauntyng, liyng, anger, coveitise;
Thise foure sparkles longen unto eelde.
Oure olde lemes mowe wel been unweelde,
But wyl ne shal nat faillen, that is sooth.
780 And yet ik have alwey a coltes tooth,
As many a yeer as it is passed henne
Syn that my tappe of lif bigan to renne.
For sikerly, whan I was bore, anon
Deeth drough the tappe of lyf and leet it gon,
785 And ever sithe hath so the tappe yronne
Til that almoost al empty is the tonne.
The streem of lyf now droppeth on the chymbe.
The sely tonge may wel rynge and chymbe
Of wrecchednesse that passed is ful yoore;
790 With olde folk, save dotage, is namoore!'
  Whan that oure Hoost hadde herd this sermonyng,
He gan to speke as lordly as a kyng.
He seide, 'What amounteth al this wit?
What shul we speke alday of hooly writ?
795 The devel made a reve for to preche,

Or of a soutere a shipman or a leche.
Sey forth thy tale, and tarie nat the tyme.
Lo Depeford, and it is half-wey pryme!
Lo Grenewych, ther many a shrewe is inne!
800   It were al tyme thy tale to bigynne.'
     'Now, sires,' quod this Osewold the Reve,
'I pray yow alle that ye nat yow greve,
Thogh I answere, and somdeel sette his howve;
For leveful is with force force of-showve.
805   'This dronke Millere hath ytoold us heer
How that bigyled was a carpenteer,
Peraventure in scorn, for I am oon.
And, by youre leve, I shal hym quite anoon;
Right in his cherles termes wol I speke.
810   I pray to God his nekke mote to-breke;
He kan wel in myn eye seen a stalke,
But in his owene he kan nat seen a balke.'

Notes

The Miller's Tale is the second of Chaucer's *Canterbury Tales*, a collection of stories told by different tellers. Chaucer organized his collection as a competition between a group of people of different occupations who had met at the Tabard inn in Southwark before setting out on the pilgrimage to Canterbury. A pilgrimage was a journey to a saint's shrine, usually undertaken to benefit the pilgrim's soul, but some people went on pilgrimages for social reasons, or for the pleasure of travel. Chaucer's pilgrims decide to increase the pleasure of their journey by holding a story-telling competition. Whoever tells tales which give best instruction (*sentence*) and most enjoyment (*solas*) will win a free meal at a grand supper to be paid for by the other pilgrims. This scheme has wonderful psychological plausibility but it also results in an interesting set of contrasts. The pilgrims are competing with each other in telling stories, but they are collaborating in making the journey more enjoyable. Some are driven primarily by religious purposes, while others have secular pleasures in view. Some try to win the competition with the morality of their teaching, while others like The Miller aim to amuse the company.

The Canterbury Tales comprises three types of material: the tales, representing the different types of medieval story (such as romances, animal fables, moral stories and saints' lives); the *General Prologue*, which describes the pilgrims and outlines Chaucer's plan; and the link passages (such as *The Miller's Prologue*), in which the pilgrims react to the tale they have just heard and prepare for the next. Chaucer's plan for *The Canterbury Tales* was left incomplete at his death, so we do not know how he would have worked out all the tensions among his pilgrims. *The Miller's Tale* is less affected by this than some others, since we can see how The Miller's personality and his reaction to *The Knight's Tale* influence his tale, and how it in turn stung The Reeve into telling his.

One of Chaucer's main techniques throughout *The Canterbury Tales* is irony. A simple definition would say that irony involves saying one thing while meaning something very different. In line 15, for example, Chaucer speaks of The Miller's 'courtesy', but since he is speaking of The Miller's refusal to defer to people, the opposite meaning 'rudeness' is implied. Much of the humour of *The Miller's Tale* results from a contradiction between words and actions or between an expression and its intended meaning. For example, courtly language may accompany an extremely vulgar action (see lines 168–73). In such a case the language (and the ideal of the class which uses it) is mocked. Sometimes a word is used mainly to mean one thing but another, more critical meaning is present in the background. In line 453 Nicholas undertakes to 'save' Alison from the flood, but his whole purpose in inventing the prophecy is to commit adultery with her, so the opposite meaning of damning her is also implied.

The Miller's Portrait: General Prologue

In the *General Prologue* Chaucer gives descriptions of all the pilgrims. Usually these mix observations about their occupations with character descriptions and moral comment. The Miller is described overwhelmingly in physical terms. He is strong and ugly, loud and foul-mouthed, and he cheats his customers. Can you find anything redeeming in this portrait? The tales Chaucer gives his pilgrims fit their descriptions in the *General Prologue* in different ways. Sometimes there is a close similarity, sometimes the tale reveals a facet of the pilgrim we could not have guessed at, and sometimes the assignation of a tale to a particular teller appears quite arbitrary. How well does *The Miller's Tale* fit in with his portrait? (See Approaches, pp. 89–91.)

545 **stout carl**   strong rogue; (*carl* has overtones of vice, like other words for the lower classes, such as churl or villein).
for the nones   indeed.
546 **brawn**   muscle.
547 **over al ther he cam**   wherever he went.
548   The ram would be the prize in the wrestling competition.
549   It is hard to reconcile *short-sholdred* with *brood* (broad) and *thikke* (sturdy). Perhaps his forearms or his neck were short while

his shoulders were broad. *Knarre* usually means 'crag', so perhaps 'rugged man'.

550 **nolde heve of harre**   would not lift off its hinges.

551 **rennyng**   running.
     heed   head.

552 **berd**   beard.
     reed   red. What is the effect of these comparisons with animals?

552–7 The medieval science of physiognomy aimed to determine people's character on the basis of their faces. In the medieval manuals red hair and large nostrils (*nosethirles* [557]) were said to indicate anger, foolishness and lechery. A large mouth suggested gluttony and boldness. See W. C. Curry, *Chaucer and the Medieval Sciences* for further details.

553 **therto**   in addition.

554 **cop**   top.

555 **werte**   wart.
     toft of herys   tuft of hairs.

556 **erys**   ears.

558 **bokeler**   small shield.
     bar   carried, wore.

559 **forneys**   oven, or perhaps cauldron.

560 **janglere**   chatterer, teller of tales.
     goliardeys   buffoon, joker.

561 **harlotries**   indecency. *That* refers to his jokes and tales.

562 **tollen thries**   take three times the accepted payment.

563 Millers judged grain with their thumbs, so a golden thumb might imply that he made large profits, but there is also an allusion to the proverb: *an honest miller hath a golden thumb* which implies that there are no honest millers.

565 **sowne**   play, sound.

The Miller's Prologue
Reactions to The Knight's Tale: Lines 1–11

When they have heard *The Knight's Tale*, all the pilgrims, both young and old, but especially those of noble birth, agree that it is a noble story and worthy to be remembered. Pleased with this opening tale,

The Host, Harry Baily, proposes that another impressive pilgrim, The Monk, who acts more like a nobleman than a priest, should tell the next. Why do you think he does this? (See Approaches p. 89.)

1 **Whan** when.
   ytoold told. In Middle English the past participle often has a *y-* prefix.
2 **route** company.
2–3 **nas ther...seyde** there was none of them either young or old who did not (*ne*) say (in Modern English, they all said it was).
3 **noble storie** The Knight told a philosophical romance, a story of two young princes who fell in love with the princess they saw from their prison window, and fought for her. Through the help (and the cruelty) of the pagan gods, Arcite won the battle but was immediately crushed by his horse, leaving his rival Palamon to marry Emily many years later. The story has a noble subject (idealistic courtly love), noble characters, and is told in a way which illustrates The Knight's understanding of the highest conventions of story-telling. The pilgrims may have considered it noble for all (or any) of these reasons. Some of them may not have reacted favourably to its 'superiority'. The basic plot situation of *The Knight's Tale* has some similarities with *The Miller's Tale* in that both concern a girl with two lovers, both involve some sort of supernatural intervention and both raise questions about the justice of fate.
4 **drawen to memorie** impress on their memories. Medieval psychology proposed that the mind had three segments, or faculties, one of which was memory.
5 **namely** especially.
   gentils those of noble birth. Who would these pilgrims be?
   everichon everyone, all of them. Is Chaucer implying that The Knight's romance was addressed more to the nobles than to the commoners?
6 **Hooste** host. Harry Baily, the innkeeper (or host) at the Tabard, has agreed to accompany the pilgrims on their journey and to preside over the story-telling competition.
   lough laughed.
   So moot I gon As I may prosper (a common medieval oath).
7 **aright** well.
   unbokeled unbuckled, opened.

male bag. The host means only that the story-telling has begun, but there may be further implications. Once a bag or a box has been opened it may be hard to close it again. Unexpected or uncontrollable things may emerge.

8 **Lat se** let us see.

10 Monks were people who swore to remove themselves from the world and devote themselves to prayer and contemplation. In the *General Prologue* The Monk is described as a jolly and manly man, a noble prelate who is preoccupied with hunting and good food. Roast swan is his favourite dish. In the medieval social hierarchy it would have seemed fitting to go from a representative of the secular ruling class (The Knight) to a high-ranking churchman.

konne know how to.

11 **quite with** reply to, but also perhaps 'repay' or 'rival'.

The Miller's Interruption: Lines 12–35

The Miller, who is already drunk and in no condition to remember his manners, interrupts The Host, declaring in a loud voice that he will tell the next tale. He brushes aside The Host's attempt to restrain him and announces that his tale will be about a carpenter, his wife, and the student who becomes her lover. What do we learn about The Miller's character? Why does he apologize for his drunkenness (29–32) when he has only just put himself forward so forcefully (16–19, 24–5)? What can we learn about The Host from his three very different speeches in *The Miller's Prologue* (6–11, 21–3, 26–7)?

12 **for dronken** because of being drunk.

13 **unnethe** hardly.

14 **nolde** (= *ne wolde*) would not.
avalen take off. The doffing of hats, and the uncovering of the head when speaking to a superior, were expected forms of politeness (compare with line 15).

15 **abyde** defer to. The mention of *his curteisie* may be ironic, in that The Miller's brand of courtesy is not courtesy at all.

16 **Pilates voys** a loud, ranting voice (suitable for playing the role of Pontius Pilate in the Mystery Plays). The Mystery Plays were a sequence of short plays telling significant episodes of Christian

history, from the creation to the last judgement. They were performed in the open air in many English towns on Corpus Christi day (one of the great festivals of the Christian calendar, which usually occurs in June) between about 1375 and 1576. The main focus of the cycle of plays was the life of Jesus Christ, and within that Pilate, the Roman governor of Palestine who condemned Christ to death, was an important villain. The nature of the role and the conditions of performance require a loud ranting voice. It is interesting that although the plays only began to be performed in his lifetime, Chaucer can already use the actors' ranting as a proverbial expression of loudness. There are several references to the Mystery Plays in *The Miller's Tale*. They may represent a conscious attempt by Chaucer to relate this tale to popular culture.

gan to crie   cried out (past tense).

17 The Miller swears by the arms, blood and bones of Christ, a blasphemous but colourful oath.

18 **kan**   know.

for the nones   for the occasion. The Miller is using the word 'noble' in an aggressively ironic sense.

19 Is The Miller merely repeating The Host's word (*quite* [11]) or is he giving it a more forceful twist? Could it be somewhat aggressive to use the same word while intending a stronger meaning?

21 **Abyd**   wait.

leeve   dear.

22 **bettre**   higher on the social scale. But perhaps, in view of line 27, The Host also privately means 'morally better'. Medieval people usually thought of the social world as very strictly organized in order of rank. The pilgrimage is one of the few occasions on which people from different classes could mix on terms of rough equality. Even on the pilgrimage The Host tries to retain some aspects of the social order. Do you think The Host means to be rude to The Miller here?

23 **werken thriftily**   act properly, arrange things fittingly. Perhaps The Miller does not accept The Host's idea of the proper way to behave.

25 **elles**   else.

go my wey   travel on my own. The Miller's threat to leave the company reminds us that The Host's authority to regulate the pilgrimage (which the pilgrims agreed to in the *General Prologue*) rests on the consent of the other pilgrims.

26 **a devel wey**   in the devil's name.

27 **wit**   reason. The Host means that drink has made The Miller irrational (in the *General Prologue* he is often compared to animals), but The Host is the one who *is overcome* in the argument.

28 **herkneth**   listen.
   alle and some   one and all, everyone.

29 **protestacioun**   solemn declaration. The word has implications of a legal plea, or of a statement denying blame. The Miller may be using it humorously.

30 From the sound of my voice I know that I am drunk.

31 **mysspeke or seye**   speak or say anything wrong (the prefix *mys-* applies to both verbs).

32 **Wyte it**   blame it on. The Tabard inn, from which the pilgrims set out earlier in the morning was in Southwark (*Southwerk*). Perhaps we should be amused that it is The Host's own beer (which he was happy to sell) that is now disrupting his plans.

33 **legende and a lyf**   story and a biography. In many contexts the phrase would suggest that the speaker intends to tell the life of a saint (a common type of story to medieval audiences).

35 **clerk**   student.
   set the wrightes cappe   deceived the carpenter. Because of the mention of the carpenter's wife in the previous line, everyone would assume (rightly) that the deception involved is adultery. Do you think this story sounds like a saint's life?

The Reeve's Objection: Lines 36–58

The Reeve urges The Miller not to speak, since he assumes that a story about a deceived carpenter will inevitably be an attack on him, because he used to be a carpenter. But The Miller pushes his objection aside, explaining that only married men can be cuckolds, that there are many virtuous women, and that the best way to avoid becoming a cuckold is not to enquire too closely into your wife's secrets. This raises two problems: the medieval (and renaissance) attitude to adultery and the implications of The Miller's rather oblique reply.

Although the Church always condemned all types of adultery (which the seventh commandment forbids [*Exodus*, 20, 14]), social attitudes to sex outside marriage were rather different. Hardly any blame was attached to young men who seduced married women (seducing a virgin was regarded as an offence). While women were blamed if they had lovers (and could sometimes suffer very severe penalties) it was almost expected that given the chance they would. This reflects both the fact that most marriages were arranged (with the result that romantic love would often only exist outside marriage) and the offensively low view which most men took of women's moral standards. The husband of the woman who took a lover was termed a cuckold (*cokewold* [44]), a figure of fun, treated with derision by his contemporaries. It seems as though it was the honour of the husband (and perhaps of the wife's brothers) that was at stake in cases of adultery. In this male-dominated society the anxiety which the men felt about the sexual fidelity of their wives was transferred into an endless series of jokes, so that (surprisingly to us) any mention of cuckolds was likely to be greeted with howls of laughter from both sexes (though for different reasons). In many medieval stories (and especially in *fabliaux* – see Notes pp. 38–9) it was expected that an old man marrying a younger woman would be made a cuckold. Nor was it any use for the husband to try to evade his fate, for the jealous husband was an equally ridiculous figure (at least in literature).

The Reeve appears to think that the honour of himself, his wife and women generally is at risk in the tale The Miller is about to tell. The Miller's reply is rather evasive. He makes three statements: first, you cannot be a cuckold if you have no wife (44); second, there are many good women for every bad one (47); and third, that it is best not to enquire too carefully into your wife's secrets (50–8). While the second appears to be reassuring, the third creates further anxiety. The first is ambiguous and The Miller pointedly refers it to the marital situation of The Reeve.

36 **Reve**   reeve, estate-manager.
   Stynt thy clappe   stop your chatter.
37 **Lat be**   let go, stop.
   lewed   ignorant (or perhaps, lascivious).
   harlotrye   crude stories, ribald talk.

38 **eek** also.

39 **apeyren** injure.
   hym defame defame him, spoil his reputation.

40 **swich** such.
   fame disrepute.

41 You may say as much as you like about other matters. Although The Reeve here says that defamation in general and slandering women are sinful, his own tale does both.

42 **spak ful soone ageyn** replied immediately.

43 What is the tone of 'dear brother' here?

44 **cokewold** cuckold, betrayed husband (see Notes pp. 33–4). This phrase may be a proverb. It states that only a husband can be a cuckold. It may also imply that all husbands are cuckolds.

45 **oon** one. What is the effect of *therfore* (for that reason)?

46 **ful** very.

47 And always a thousand good ones for every bad one. The Miller's expression looks like borrowed wisdom. Chaucer uses almost the same phrase in the Prologue to *The Legend of Good Women* (G text, line 277). It also appears in *The Mirror of Marriage* by the French poet Eustache Deschamps (?1340–1406).

48 **knowestow** (= *thou knowest*) you know.
   but if thou madde unless you are mad.

49 **artow** (= *art thou*) are you.
   tale words, talk.

50 **pardee** certainly. Although this oath originally meant 'by God', its force had become weakened by familiarity.
   as wel as thow as much as you, just as you have.

51 **nolde** (= *ne wolde*) would not want. The Miller regards the oxen in his plough team as valuable possessions which he would not want to lose. Some critics think there may be a link between the horns of the oxen and the (proverbial) horns of the cuckold.

52–3 Take upon myself the extra burden (literally, more than enough) of believing that I am one (that is, a cuckold).

54 **wol bileve wel** shall firmly believe.
   noon not one, none.

55 **nat** not.
   inquisityf inquisitive, curious.

56 About God's secrets (*pryvetee*) or those of a wife. Medieval Christians believed that it was not up to human beings to question God's reasons. But *pryvetee* can also mean 'private

parts', and the next line makes it clear that The Miller intends the pun, warning married men that as long as they have satisfaction from their wives, they should not enquire too much about their wives' other sexual activities.

57 **So** as long as, provided that.

foyson plenty. There is a very striking (not to say shocking) contrast here between the theological phrase 'God's plenty' and what it refers to (sexual activity).

58 There is no need (*nedeth nat*) to enquire about the rest (*remenant*).

Chaucer's Apology: Lines 59–78

Chaucer ends *The Miller's Prologue* by speaking in his own voice, as the narrator of the whole *Canterbury Tales*. He warns his readers that The Miller and The Reeve are scoundrels who are going to tell dirty stories, and advises those who want a more improving tale to read a different one. Do you think that Chaucer is really trying to spare the embarrassment of his more pious readers? Is it, as Alfred David says in his book *The Strumpet Muse*, 'an obvious come-on' designed to attract readers? Or is Chaucer simply trying to avoid responsibility for what he has written? It is worth remembering that until recently many readers did 'turn the page' (69), regarding *The Miller's Tale* as unfit for proper discussion or serious study.

60 He would not restrain (*forbere*) his words out of respect for anyone.

61 **cherles** churl's, rascal's. Churl was a descriptive term for the lowest class in medieval society. The word was also used to describe immoral or impolite behaviour. Some of these meanings survive in the Modern English word 'churlish'. In general Chaucer uses this common word rather infrequently, so the two occurrences (61, 74) here might imply strong condemnation. On the other hand Chaucer might be questioning the applicability of the word, asking what it means if we dismiss The Miller and The Reeve as churls.

manere manner, own way.

62 **M'athynketh** it displeases me, I regret.

reherce relate, repeat.

63 **gentil** noble, well-born. Just as terms describing the lower class were used to convey negative sentiments, so *gentil* came to signify positive qualities, such as compassion, sensitivity and goodness. *Gentillesse* (71), a key medieval term whose implications are debated in *The Canterbury Tales*, denoted both the behaviour appropriate to someone of noble birth and virtuous action more generally. *Gentil* could also be used as a polite (or flattering) form of address.

    wight person.

64 **demeth nat that I seye** do not think that I speak.

65 **Of yvel entente** with an evil intention.

66 **Hir** their.

    bettre better (probably he means morally better).

67 **falsen** falsify.

    mateere subject-matter. As in the *General Prologue* (725–42), Chaucer explains that he has no wish to write down the crude story which follows, but his obligation to tell the truth about the pilgrimage compels him to.

68 **whoso list it nat yheere** whoever does not wish to hear it. This line implies an audience of listeners, the next line an audience of readers. Both types of audience were possible at the time. The poet might declaim his poem before the court, but manuscript copies were made which others could read to themselves, or to an audience of their family and friends.

69 **leef** page.

    chese choose.

70 **ynowe** enough.

71 Historical (*storial*) matter concerning noble behaviour (*gentillesse*, see Note to line 63 above). Chaucer would probably have regarded some of the moral legends (such as *The Sergeant of the Law's Tale* and *The Second Nun's Tale*) as historical.

73 **amys** wrongly.

75 **mo** more.

76 **harlotrie** crude stories.

77 **Avyseth yow** Consider this.

78 **maken ernest of game** take as serious (*ernest*) what is playful (*game*). *Ernest* and *game* (joke) are proverbial opposites in Middle English, but Chaucer often makes jokes about things he means seriously. What guidance is Chaucer giving us about how to read *The Miller's Tale*? Can we trust it?

The Miller's Tale

The Miller's Tale belongs to the genre of the *fabliau* (plural *fabliaux*). *Fabliaux* are defined as 'short funny stories in the vernacular' (that is in the local language of everyday speech, rather than in Latin, the universal learned language). They usually involve an act of deception and a misdeed, usually connected with sex or excretion. The *fabliaux* contain a fairly restricted cast of characters: a cunning woman (who may trick either her husband or a prospective lover), a prostitute, a jealous old husband, a lecherous student, a merchant or a priest. The characters are usually not developed as individuals, but are defined by their gender and their social position. Usually one of the group (in most cases the husband) is victimized and humiliated by some of the others. Scholars have been able to identify three types of *fabliau* (crudely, the second flood, the misdirected kiss, and the branding) which Chaucer combined in order to produce the plot of *The Miller's Tale*. Most of the *fabliaux* which survive are written in Old French, and were composed in northern France between about 1190 and 1340. There are also several German *fabliaux* from the Thirteenth century, and a few in Dutch. (It is in fact possible that the Dutch/Flemish *fabliaux* are earlier than the French ones.) There is considerable debate about the audience of the *fabliaux*. Some writers see them as an anarchic and popular form of literature, while others think they were an aristocratic form (a way of looking down on the peasants), pointing out that they are often found in expensive manuscripts, and that if noble characters appear they are never the victims. Students often appear in the *fabliaux* and usually get the better of other characters. That Chaucer, who wrote most of the *fabliaux* in Middle English, always gives them to lower class tellers may indicate that he regarded the form as popular. (For further discussion of the *fabliau* see Approaches pp. 91–3 and the examples in the Appendix pp. 166–7.)

For the moment it is important to mention that while Chaucer adapted the form (for example, by introducing far more characterization and a considerable amount of parody) he also abided by most of its basic assumptions (many of which we would regard as sexist). In a *fabliau* it was expected that students would be lecherous, that young wives would take lovers, and that old husbands would be jealous and become cuckolds. We must be alert for the variations which Chaucer plays on these themes, rather than expecting him to do without them.

Introduction and Portrait of Nicholas: Lines 79–112

The tale opens, in an apparently leisurely way, with descriptions of the main characters. These descriptions abound in details of fourteenth century life, but they also convey a good deal of information and expectation on which the plot will later depend. Nicholas is a student, but his main interest is in astrology. He is an expert in 'secret love' and a fine musician. We learn about his character from a tour of his room, which contains herbs, stones, textbooks, scientific equipment, and a musical instrument, the psaltery. Do these tell us more about his studies or his hobbies? In fact the description of Nicholas is rather like the thumbnail sketches of the pilgrims in the *General Prologue*. It might be interesting to compare it with those of The Miller (see p. 1) and The Clerk (see p. 163). What conclusions should we draw from Nicholas' combination of foresight, secrecy, love and music? (See Approaches, pp. 103–06.)

79 **Whilom** Once. *Whilom ther was* is almost as traditional an opening formula as the Modern English 'Once upon a time'.
   Oxenford Oxford. J. A. W. Bennett shows that the main background details from *The Miller's Tale* can be paralleled (and brought to life) from Oxford's historical records (*Chaucer at Oxford and Cambridge*, pp. 26–57). Although this does not prove that Chaucer knew Oxford well, it demonstrates the realism of the tale.

80 **gnof** churl, lout. This is the only occurrence of the word in Middle English literature, which may mean that it was a colloquial term of abuse. (It also implies that this meaning, which scholars agree on, must be regarded as a guess only.) The carpenter is rich enough to have a servant and a maid as well as a large house, but he still does manual work.
   gestes heeld to bord took in lodgers.

81 **craft** trade.

82 **poure scoler** poor scholar. This may represent a formula often found in legal documents, or it may (in view of Nicholas' expensive possessions) be ironic.

83 **art** the arts course. In medieval universities, all students studied the arts course (which in theory consisted of all seven liberal arts [grammar, logic, rhetoric, arithmetic, geometry, music and astronomy], but in practice concentrated mainly on logic) before going on to one of the higher faculties (law, medicine and theology). Since the description mentions no higher faculty but emphasizes astrology, presumably Nicholas is still studying the arts course. But the word 'art' can be applied to astrology (see line 101), so Chaucer may be using the same word to denote his official and his actual studies.

   fantasye imagination, desire.

84 **turned** directed. In the Middle Ages astrology (*astrologye*) was not completely distinguished from astronomy. The position of the stars at someone's birth was widely believed to influence character, and the movements of the planets were thought to cause changes in emotions and even the onset of diseases. In some respects this is similar to modern interest in horoscopes, but it also went further in that a good deal of medical practice depended on the position of the stars (see the description of The Doctor of Physic in the *General Prologue*). Although many of these practices were tolerated, the Church was opposed to attempts to foretell the future on the basis of the stars, which is what Nicholas is interested in. In his *Treatise on the Astrolabe*, Chaucer states his disbelief in astrological prediction (*Riverside Chaucer*, p. 671), but in his poems he often introduces changes of weather (see line 88) with reference to the position of the stars. Like other Christian poets exploiting myths about the pagan Gods, he may have regarded this as a matter more of poetic practice than of belief.

85 And understood (*koude*) some (*a certeyn*) of the propositions (*conclusiouns*). The implication is that Nicholas' knowledge of the art is limited. He knows (or thinks he knows) how to predict some things but not others.

86 **demen** judge, decide.

   interrogaciouns questions.

87 **certein houres** the exact time.

88 **droghte or elles shoures** dry weather or rain. Apparently the carpenter believes in Nicholas' ability to predict the weather (see lines 406–14).

89 **bifalle** happen.

90 **rekene** count.

hem them.

91 The word *clerk* has a range of uses. Any learned man, or anyone who was studying beyond the elementary level could be called a *clerk*. But the word could also be used more strictly of the priesthood (clergy). When Absolon is called a *parissh clerk* though, he is neither a student nor a priest but an assistant to the priest. (See line 204.)

cleped called.

hende courteous. This word is used eleven times in the tale. *The Oxford English Dictionary* lists a range of meanings: 'near, at hand; handy, ready or skilful with the hand; pleasant in dealing with others; courteous, gracious; nice'. Critics have suggested that Chaucer plays with all these meanings at different points in the tale.

92 **deerne** secret.

solas pleasure, delight (perhaps with sexual implications here).

93 **sleigh** sly, cunning.

privee discreet, secretive. We should also remember the puns on *pryvetee* (56).

94 **meke** gentle, submissive, innocent. Here the emphasis is on appearance (*to see*). *Mayden* can mean a virgin of either sex. (See Approaches, p. 134.)

95 **chambre** bedroom. *Hostelrye* usually means inn or pub, but can also be used of student lodgings or a large house (Compare with *in* [439]).

96 Nicholas has a room to himself. This is required by the plot, but it may also be an indication of his wealth, since medieval students usually shared rooms. This line repeats a line from *The Knight's Tale*, which describes Arcite's tragic feeling of loneliness as death approaches:

> What is this world? What asketh men to have?
> Now with his love, now in his colde grave
> Allone, withouten any compaignye.   (2777–79)

The Miller's use of this line may be deliberate parody, or the repetition might be accidental. The phrase also appears in Chaucer's *Tale of Melibee* (line 1560).

97 Very handsomely decorated with sweet-smelling herbs.

99 **lycorys**   liquorice.

    cetewale   setwall, zedoary (a spice resembling ginger).

100 **Almageste**   astronomy textbook. *Almagest* is the common medieval title for the great astronomy textbook of the Greek scientist Claudius Ptolomaeus (Ptolemy), who was active between 127 and 148 AD. This title derives from an Arabic adaptation of the work's Greek nickname *megistee* (meaning 'the greatest'). This is a neat illustration of the way that Greek scientific knowledge was preserved and cultivated by Islamic scientists before being passed back via Islamic Spain to medieval western Europe. In the later Middle Ages *Almagest* became a generic term for the astronomy textbook, so Nicholas owned an astronomy textbook, which may or may may not have been Ptolemy's book. Ptolemy also wrote a famous textbook of astrology, the *Tetrabiblos*. Books (all of which had to be copied by hand) were extremely expensive in the Middle Ages, so Nicholas' library of large and small books indicates wealth.

101 An astrolabe (*astrelabie*) is a scientific instrument, a set of flat circular metal plates, with two pointers, which can be used to measure the position of the planets. For his son Lewis, Chaucer wrote *A Treatise on the Astrolabe*, which describes the construction and use of the instrument. Although astrolabes are not rare, relatively few students would have owned one. (See photograph of an astrolabe on p. 142.)

    longynge for   belonging to.

102 **augrym stones**   counting stones. These were stones or counters with Arabic numerals on them, which could be placed on a marked board and used as a type of abacus.

    faire apart   neatly on their own.

103 **couched**   placed.

104 **presse**   cupboard.

    faldyng   coarse woollen cloth.

105 **al above**   on top of everything.

    gay   elegant. A psaltery (*sautrie*) was a stringed instrument like a small harp. The Clerk in the *General Prologue*, who is rather different from Nicholas, would rather have philosophy books than an elegant psaltery (line 296). What does this tell us about Nicholas' priorities?

108 *Angelus ad virginem* (Latin, meaning 'The angel to the virgin') is the first line, and therefore the title, of a well-known song about the Annunciation, the episode in the *Bible* in which the angel Gabriel visits the Virgin Mary to tell her that she has been chosen to give birth to God's son Jesus. (Modern recordings of this song have been released, including one by The Tallis Scholars.) Do you think we should take this as evidence of Nicholas' religious devotion, or is there an irony in view of his behaviour later in the tale? (See Approaches, p. 124.)
   song sung.

109 **the Kynges Noote** the King's tune (probably a popular song of the time but not so far firmly identified).

110 **myrie** tuneful. Do you think this line means that he sang a lot, or that those who heard him often blessed him for his songs?

111 Why is he a *sweete clerk*?

112 **After** according to.
   freendes fyndyng the gifts of his friends.
   rente income. Do you think there might be some criticism here? The portrait of The Clerk in the *General Prologue* (lines 299–302, see p. 163) also refers to the friends who subsidize his studies.

The Carpenter's Marriage: Lines 113–124

The carpenter is used as a point of departure for both portraits. Nicholas is his lodger, and Alison is his wife. The marriage is recent; the wife young and 'wild' (*wylde* [117]), the husband old and jealous (*Jalous* [116]). The Miller allows himself a few conventional comments (and a not very learned quotation) on the problems of marriage. Perhaps the passage encourages us to think of John and Alison at first as 'types', a view which will be modified as the tale proceeds. (See Approaches pp. 99–101, 107–08.)

113 **newe** recently. Strictly *wyf* means 'woman' (as opposed to maiden), but here (and throughout this tale) 'wife' seems the most appropriate modern equivalent.

116 **heeld hire narwe in cage** kept her closely confined. It appears

that the *cage* here is metaphorical; there are French *fabliaux* in which it is literal.

117 Why is she called *wylde*? Do you think that this is The Miller's prejudice and that really she is just young (*yong*), or is she already being likened to an animal?

118 Do you think *been lik* means 'likely to become' or just 'like'?

119 Cato (*Catoun*) here refers to the book of short proverbs which was used in medieval schools as the most elementary Latin reader. If you had not read 'Cato', you had not read anything. No doubt the book derived some of its prestige from a supposed link with the Roman Cato the elder (234–149 BC), famous for the pithy expression of traditional moral values.
   rude   uneducated, ignorant.

120 **bad**   advised.
   his simylitude   someone like him.

121 **after hire estaat**   according to their position (here, in age; usually, in society).

122 **elde**   old age.
   at debaat   at odds, quarrelling. This expression is proverbial. It also expresses a continuing theme of *The Canterbury Tales*.

123 **sith**   since. Why does The Miller call marriage a *snare*? Should we link this with the *cage* (116)?

124 **care**   trouble. Does this expression denote sympathy or is it generalized and empty? Is The Miller philosophical or smug?

Portrait of the Carpenter's Wife: Lines 125–62

The detailed description of the heroine was an important set-piece in the romance, and a subject for courtly love lyrics. In this description Chaucer seems to be parodying such poetic portraits, comparing the carpenter's wife (from now on I shall call her Alison, but we do not actually learn her name until line 258) with the domestic and everyday, where the court poets would have chosen exotic and valuable objects of comparison. (See Approaches, pp. 107–08.)

Should we see the portrait as an amusing parody, as an image of wholesome sexuality, or as a shameless fantasy of a woman's body presented for the amusement of a male audience? Charles Muscatine

(*Chaucer and the French Tradition*, p. 229) points out that although Chaucer adapts and parodies the conventions of courtly descriptions, he still follows the same set of categories:

the fairness, the eye, the bent brows, the hue, the voice, the mouth, the carriage, the silken costume, the jewelry, the accomplishments.

125 **Fair** beautiful.

therwithal besides, also.

126 **wezele** weasel.

gent delicate.

smal slender. What are the implications of this unusual comparison?

127 She wore (*werede*) a belt (*ceynt*) decorated with strips (*barred*) entirely (*al*) of silk. Just possibly *al* could qualify *barred*, and mean 'all over'.

128 **barmclooth** apron.

whit white.

morne morning.

129 **lendes** loins.

goore fold, flounce.

130 **smok** shift, slip (worn under the apron, and visible above it).

130-1 **broyden...coler** embroidered all over the front (*bifoore*) and back (*bihynde*) and around the collar (*coler*). The punctuation here is by the modern editor. If it were removed, the clothes would have to be understood differently (for example, one might take the collar as black, rather than the embroidery).

132 With black silk, both inside and outside. If the collar is open, then embroidery on the inside could be seen. Should we think of the expense of all the embroidery on this white *smok* (130) or of the attention it attracts? What is the effect of the pervasive and strong contrast of black and white?

133 **tapes** ribbons (which hold her cap [*voluper*] in place).

134 **suyte** pattern.

135 **filet brood** wide headband. It is placed very high to show off her forehead.

136 **sikerly** certainly.

likerous ye lustful eye.

137 **Ful smale ypulled** very finely plucked.

138 **tho** those.

bent   curved, arched.
blake   black.
sloo   sloe-berry.

139 **blisful**   delightful.
on to see   to look on.

140 **pere-jonette**   early ripening pear.

141 Is there any reason for thinking that the wool (*wolle*) of the male sheep (*wether*) is especially soft? How soft is Alison and in what way?

142 **girdel**   belt.
heeng   hung.

143 **perled...latoun**   decorated with brass beads.

144 **to seken...doun**   wherever you might look.

145 **nys**   (= *ne is*) is not (but the whole phrase means 'is no man', see A Note on Chaucer's English, p. 148).
thenche   think, imagine. It would be an ordinary compliment to say: 'nowhere in the world is there any woman like her'; but after setting up this expectation, The Miller first frustrates it (no *man*), and then produces an even more extreme statement (nowhere in the world is there anyone so wise [*wys*] as to be able to imagine her). This is an example of witty hyperbole, which is also self deflating, since Alison is an imaginary construction of Chaucer's.

146 Such a joyful pet or such a wench. After such a build up neither expression is exactly complimentary. *Popelote* (poppet) suggests a doll, beautiful and undemanding, while *wenche* implies coarseness and sexual availability. (See Approaches, p. 127.)

147 **hewe**   colouring, complexion.

148 **Tour**   Tower of London, where coins, including the noble (worth a third of a pound sterling) were minted (*yforged*). This expression seems to draw together (partly through wordplay) some of the themes of the description so far: cages, newness, brightness, money, and social status (noble/wench). It continues the tendency to compare her with valuable (and exchangeable?) objects.

149 **yerne**   lively. Alison's voice is stronger than a courtly lady's would be.

150 **swalwe**   swallow.
berne   barn.

151 **Therto**   in addition, moreover.
make game   gambol, be playful.

152 **dame** mother.

153 **bragot** bragget (an alcoholic drink made by fermenting ale and honey).

meeth mead (fermented honey and water). What is the effect of talking about Alison's taste and comparing her with sweet intoxicating drinks? Perhaps there is poetry in the physicality of these comparisons.

154 **hoord** store.

heeth heather. But we do not know that people stored apples in heather.

155 **Wynsynge** skittish, lively.

joly high-spirited, frisky.

156 As tall as a mast and as straight as a bolt (of a crossbow).

157–8 On her low-cut collar she wore a brooch which was as wide as the boss of a shield (*bokeler*). Or perhaps the collar is low because it is open (see Note to line 132, p. 45). Why would Alison wear a large brooch here?

160 Both *prymerole* (primrose) and *piggesnye* (pig's eye) are flowers. They emphasize Alison's passive beauty and again associate her with the natural world. Or we could think of both words as affectionate names.

161 **leggen** lay.

162 In a spirit of realism, The Miller suggests different ways in which she could trade on her beauty: by marrying an honest free-born man (*good yeman*), probably a little above her in the social scale; or by briefly becoming the mistress of someone much more important, a lord. Does this imply criticism or admiration of the different choice (marrying a fairly rich old tradesman) she has in fact made?

Nicholas Molests Alison: Lines 163–98

After describing two of his four main characters, The Miller sets his plot in motion. Nicholas takes advantage of the carpenter's absence to declare his love for Alison, and to grab hold of her thighs. With a short protest, and a little persuasion she grants him her love, and they agree to trick the carpenter.

The comedy of this passage depends on a contrast between Nicholas' very rude actions and his use of the elaborate and polite language of courtly romance. In courtly romances and love-lyrics, the lover tended to present himself as the inferior of his lady, as her worshipper and her servant. He spoke of the pain he felt, almost amounting to death, and (in religious terms) of his need of her mercy. Conventionally the lover made a secret of his affection, so as not to compromise his lady's honour. Although such lovers always pretended an entirely selfless devotion, content to admire the lady and to receive the occasional kind glance in return, in practice most of them aimed at a sexual relationship. This means that Nicholas' inappropriate use of the language of courtly romance (169–80) is an exposé of the truth (in that the courtier-lovers pretend to be pure but are really like Nicholas) as well as a witty parody. Audiences accustomed to *fabliaux* would probably have been amused rather than outraged by Nicholas' behaviour in this context. You may disagree.

163 **eft**   again.
   so bifel the cas   it so happened.
164 **on a day**   one day. On *hende* (courteous) see Note to line 91, p. 41.
165 **Fil**   began.
   rage   sport (with a sexual sense, as there is also in *pleye* here). (See Approaches, p. 97.)
166 **Oseneye**   Osney, now a part of Oxford, but then a village outside, with a large abbey, where the carpenter often worked, as we learn later on (553–60).
167 **ful queynte**   very sly. Why *As* (since)?
168 **prively**   secretly. There is no doubt about where Nicholas grabs her. *Queynte* means 'elegant, pleasing thing' and is used as a euphemism for vagina. There may be a pun on the similar sounding 'cunt', as vulgar in Middle English as it is today.
169–70 **Ywis...spille**   Indeed, unless I obtain what I desire, my love (*lemman*), I shall die (*spille*) for secret love of you. *Lemman, derne* and *spille* are common words in courtly love poetry, but there the lover would not make his threat (the same one) so promptly, or with Nicholas' accompanying action. Some critics regard *spille* as an obscene pun, since it can also mean 'ejaculate'.
171 **haunchebones**   thighs.
172 **al atones**   at once, immediately.

173 **also...save** God preserve me.

174 **sproong** leaped, sprang.

   trave frame in which unruly horses were restrained while they were shod. How is this image appropriate to Alison and her situation?

175 **wryed** twisted. Alison twisted her head (*heed*) rapidly away from Nicholas to make it more difficult for him to kiss her.

176 **by my fey** on my honour. Notice that Alison here uses the familiar form (*thee* – see A Note on Chaucer's English p. 147). This form can express intimacy, a sense of superiority (a person would say 'thee' to inferiors, but 'you' to superiors), or scorn. Which do you think Alison intends here? You may find it interesting to pay attention to the way she switches between familiar and polite forms.

177 **lat be** stop, give over.

   quod said.

178 *Harrow*, *out* and *allas* are all cries of distress. Notice that Alison threatens to cry out, rather than simply doing so.

179 Take your hands off, for goodness sake.

180 In his role of courtly lover Nicholas begged (*gan...crye*) for pity from his lady. But there is a satirical contrast between the language and the situation here, where Nicholas is molesting Alison, and she asks him to stop.

181 And spoke so graciously (*faire*) and offered his love so insistently (*faste*).

183 Perhaps we should regard Alison's oath (*ooth*) as a reminder of the purpose of the pilgrimage.

184 **comandement** command, disposal.

185 **leyser** opportunity.

186 What evidence do we have of the carpenter's jealousy (*jalousie*)?

187 That unless (*but*) you watch (*wayte*) carefully and are secretive (*privee*).

188 **woot** know.

   I nam but deed I am as good as dead (literally, I am nothing but dead).

190 **therof care thee noght** do not worry about that.

191–2 A student would have wasted his time (literally, spent his time badly [*litherly*]) if he did not know how to deceive a carpenter. (See Approaches p. 118.)

193 **accorded** agreed.

194 **wayte** watch for, await. The implication of their agreement is that they will wait for a better opportunity. (See Approaches p. 105.)

195 **everideel** all, every part.

196 **thakked** patted.
 lendes loins.
 weel well.

197 **sawtrie** psaltery (see Note to line 105, p. 42).

198 **faste** rapidly, or perhaps intensely. Some critics have suggested that music in this tale serves as a codeword for sexual activity (compare lines 106 and 544). But any such interpretation of this line must take account of the implication of line 194.

Portrait of Absolon: Lines 199–230

Just when we thought *The Miller's Tale* was a simple story of adultery, Chaucer introduces his complicating factor, a second admirer for Alison. There is a large social gulf between the two lovers. Nicholas has income (112) and leisure to pursue his hobbies (84, 92, 105), where Absolon has to work for his living (204). His accomplishments are less intellectual and more practical: shaving, basic surgery, legal drafting and dancing (218–22). What do you make of the contrast between their musical skills (105–10, 223–8)? Should we regard Absolon's accomplishments as comic, or should we respect him as a 'self-made man'? (See Approaches pp. 108–111.)

Where Absolon's accomplishments reflect the real world of fourteenth-century Oxford parish clerks, his name is very uncommon, and may well refer to the Biblical Absalom (*2 Samuel*, 13–18). In the *Bible* Absalom is notable for fair but treacherous speech, and for his beauty, especially his luxuriant hair (chapter 14, verses 25–6). His hair caused his downfall because it caught in a tree allowing his pursuers to catch up with him. The description of Absolon in the tale is unusual (for a description of a man) in the amount of physical detail it provides (206–16). As with the portrait of Alison it may be helpful to think of it as a parody of the description of a courtly lady which one would expect to find in a romance (see Appendix pp. 164–5). There is discussion of his squeamishness and possible effeminacy in the Approaches p. 127.

200 To perform Christ's own works. That is, to worship God in the way Christ ordered. What is the effect of the contrast with the previous paragraph?

201 **haliday** holy day. 'Holiday' derives from this, since on holy days (Sundays and religious festivals) most people did not work.

202 **shoon** shone.

203 **leet** left, stopped. As today, the homeworker's holiday only begins when the domestic chores are finished. Notice how narrative serves characterization here. Alison goes to the church only in order that we can meet Absolon. Nothing happens until the portrait has been completed.

204 The *parissh clerk* was an assistant to the priest, who helped in various ways in the church services.

206 **Crul** curly.
     heer hair.

207 **strouted as a fanne** spread out like a fan.

208 **evene** smooth.
     shode parting (of his hair). The word *joly* (here, pretty) is often applied to Absolon. Some critics find that the word has associations with sexuality.

209 **reed** red. Both the word *rode* (complexion) and eyes (*eyen*) as grey as a goose are usually found in descriptions of heroines. (Compare Appendix p. 164, line 546.)

210 **Poules wyndow** the window of St Paul's Cathedral. Absolon's shoes have an elaborate design cut out (*corven*) on them (perhaps in the form of a second layer of leather). Presumably the design is a lattice or a circle, like a rose window. The window in question would have belonged to the old cathedral, destroyed by fire in 1666.

211 **hoses rede** red stockings.
     fetisly elegantly. We also find this word in descriptions of courtly ladies.

212 He was dressed (*Yclad*) very delicately (*smal*) and neatly (*proprely*).

213 **kirtel** tunic.
     waget sky-blue.

214 It had many beautiful laces (literally the laces [*poyntes*] were placed thickly [*thikke*] and very beautifully [*faire*]).

215 **therupon** on top of it (the tunic).

gay surplys bright (or fine) robe. Nowadays, the surplice is a loose outer robe which only priests wear.

216 **blosme upon the rys** blossom on the bough. This simile recalls the description of Alison.

217 **so God me save** as God may preserve me (a common and very weak oath). *Child* (lad) has connotations of forcefulness, vigour. Is this ironic or is Absolon a simpleton?

218 He knew well how to let blood, trim hair and shave. As well as being a parish clerk (only a part-time occupation), Absolon fulfils the duties of a barber. In the Middle Ages bloodletting was a common medical procedure. Medieval doctors usually restricted themselves to the theoretical aspects of medicine (diagnosis and formulating a cure); the practical surgery was left to a barber working to the doctor's instructions. Absolon has mastered an important practical skill, which also indicates the intellectual and social distance between him and Nicholas.

219 And draw documents of land tenure or the release of property (*acquitaunce*). Another example of a practical skill separate from the theoretical law teaching of the university. It might be significant that Absolon has practical skills corresponding to all three higher faculties of the university (see Note to line 83, p. 40).

220 **twenty** a large number (rather than exactly twenty).

221 **scole** style. But school can also mean university. Perhaps there is a joke in the apparent seriousness with which The Miller distinguishes styles of dancing. Or perhaps Chaucer is making a joke about the preoccupations of the students.

tho at that time, then.

222 **casten** leap, fling.

223 **rubible** rebec, a small two-stringed fiddle.

224 **Therto** to it (that is, with the rebec accompanying).

quynyble high treble. Either Absolon is singing falsetto or his voice has not yet broken.

225 **giterne** gittern, a small plucked four- or five-stringed instrument, the forerunner of the renaissance guitar.

226 **nas** (= *ne was*) was not. This negative cancels out with *ne* (nor). Absolon visited all the pubs with lively barmaids.

brewhous pub. Most medieval pubs brewed their own beer.

227 **solas** entertainment.

228 **gaylard tappestere** lively barmaid.

229 **sooth**   truth.
   somdeel squaymous   somewhat squeamish.
230 **of speche daungerous**   fastidious of speech (or perhaps, sparing
   of speech). Absolon likes to sing in pubs with lively barmaids,
   but he does not care for all the gross behaviour he comes across
   in them. Notice how the lines speed up to describe his music
   and dancing, whereas the concluding reservation holds them
   back.

Absolon Begins to Woo Alison: Lines 231–61

While he is swinging the censer filled with incense around the
church, Absolon has the chance to admire the women of the parish.
He is so strongly attracted to Alison that he takes his gittern out to
serenade her early the next morning, waking her and her husband.
The exaggeratedly courteous behaviour of the lover makes a comic
contrast with the religious duties he exploits (and neglects), and the
realities of fourteenth-century town life. It may be courtesy on
Absolon's part not to accept any payment, but what he is actually
refusing is the offering which will provide bread for the poor. It may
be amorous to stay up all night and sing lovesongs, but it will not do
any good if (as he must) he wakes up his mistress' husband.

231 **jolif**   lively, sprightly.
232 **sencer**   censer (the vessel containing the burning incense, like
   a kettle on the end of a chain).
233 Vigorously (*faste*) spreading incense over the women of the
   parish. There were religious festivals which only the women
   would have attended, or perhaps Absolon directs himself
   particularly to their (segregated) part of the church.
234 **lovely**   loving.
236 To stare at her seemed to him a happy pastime.
237 **propre**   beautiful.
   likerous   delightful, attractive (or perhaps flirtatious).
239 **hire hente anon**   pounce on her at once. Perhaps this violent
   simile reveals Absolon's true attitude to Alison.
241 **love-longynge**   passionate desire (an expression often found in
   medieval lovesongs).
242–3 That he would not accept an offering from any of the women.

Out of courtesy he said that he did not want any. Courtesy is ambiguous here, meaning both 'politeness' and 'sense of himself as a courtly lover'.

244 **ful brighte shoon** shone very brightly.

245 **ytake** taken.

246 Because he intended to stay up all night (*wake*) for the sake of love.

247 *Jolif* here means 'full of desire', rather than 'pretty'. Consider the other meanings of this word (also spelt *joly*), as is applied to Absolon (lines 208, 231, 240, 263).

249 **ycrowe** crowed.

250 **dressed hym** placed himself.

shot-wyndowe hinged window (a window that shuts). Most medieval windows did not open at all, but this story requires one that does (619). In fact it is hinged at the top (632, 693). This is an example of the way in which the realistic descriptions of the early part of the tale prepare elements which will be needed for the plot later.

252 **gentil and smal** fine and high-pitched.

253 **if thy wille be** if it is your wish.

254 **rewe** take pity (a typical expression of courtly love-poetry).

255 **acordaunt to** in harmony with.

gyternynge gittern-playing (see line 225).

256 **awook** awoke.

258 **Herestow nat** Do you not hear? This is the first mention of Alison's name.

259 **chaunteth thus** sings like this.

oure boures wal wall of our bedroom. Why does John ask this question?

260 **therwithal** at that.

261 **it every deel** every part of it. This line conveys Alison's lack of interest.

Absolon's Methods of Wooing: Lines 262–88

The Miller leaves the scene by the bedroom window unresolved (it will be repeated and resolved at lines 586–702), moving on to a general description of Absolon's attempts to court Alison. We should probably see this as a parody of the behaviour of a noble lover. Thus while Absolon suffers for love (feeling miserable and being unable to sleep [264–5]) and approaches his lady through an intermediary (267) as the noble lover would, his display of accomplishments (269, 276) and the gifts he offers (270–2) are very different, reflecting the difference in wealth and opportunities. Notice how the repeating sentence structure and the sequence of verbs depict the energy and resourcefulness of Absolon's wooing. But all his efforts are doomed to failure. Alison loves courteous or close-at-hand Nicholas, and treats Absolon as a figure of fun. Do we laugh at Absolon with her or do we have some understanding for his predicament? If Absolon seems to be following a model of love which is inappropriate to his social position, what do we make of The Miller's views about 'normal' amatory behaviour (273–4, 284–5)?

262　This continues: what more do you want to know? (literally, 'what do you want better than good?').

264　Woos (*woweth*) her so much that he becomes miserable (*hym is wo bigon*).

265　**waketh**　remains awake. Chaucer treats this as a typical symptom of love in the *General Prologue* (lines 10, 98).

266　**kembeth**　combs.
　　　made hym gay　made himself look handsome (or perhaps joyful).

267　**meenes**　intermediaries, middlemen (but the word can also mean 'trick' or 'bribe').
　　　brocage　use of an agent. These words convey an idea of underhand trickery, but there may also be an element of parody, since the courtly lover would usually be so overcome by love that he could only approach his lady through a friend. Absolon may be paying his broker, and in any case we should contrast this with Nicholas' more direct (and more successful) approach.

268　Absolon here imitates the courtly lover, who would offer to serve his lady to show her superiority to him, and his willingness to humble himself. Absolon ranks below a page, and Alison is not noble enough to have one.

269　**brokkynge**　warbling, trilling.
　　　as　like.

270　**pyment**　spiced wine. Absolon brings her mead (*meeth*), but The Miller says she tastes like it (153).

271 And cakes (*wafres*), whistling hot out of the embers (*gleede*). The cakes would have been baked close to the fire in the oven.

272 **profred** offered.

meede reward, money. Is The Miller casting aspersions on the morals of town girls? A medieval country girl might have less use for money.

273 **wonnen for** won, or seduced, through.

274 **strokes** blows. Should we take this as The Miller expressing generalized wisdom (in the sense of 'everyone has different tastes') or does this phrase betray his attitude to women?

275 **lightnesse** agility.

maistrye skill (but the word can also mean dominance).

276 Herod (*Herodes*) was one of the most famous roles in the Mystery Plays (see Note to line 16, pp. 31–2), celebrated for the ranting and raving it involved (hence Hamlet's complaint about exaggerated acting: *it out-herods Herod*, *Hamlet*, 3.2.15). Do you think Absolon's voice and manner suit this type of role? Mystery Plays could be acted on a platform (*scaffold*) or on a pageant wagon.

277 **what availleth hym** what does it profit him, what good does it do him? Notice how this section deflates the mood of the previous lines.

278 **hende** courteous (see Note to line 91, p. 41).

279 **blowe the bukkes horn** blow his horn, go whistle (a proverbial expression indicating that his efforts are futile).

280 He got nothing for his trouble (*labour*) but contempt, derision (*scorn*).

281 **ape** fool.

282 And turns all his seriousness (*ernest*) to (*til*) a joke (*jape*). Compare with line 78.

283 Perhaps the emphasis (*Ful sooth*) here leads us to doubt the truth of the proverb.

284 **right thus** just so, exactly like this.

nye slye near-by crafty one.

285 Makes the farther off (*ferre*) loved one (*leeve*) to be disliked (*looth*).

286 For even if Absolon should be mad (*wood*) or angry (*wrooth*).

287 **By cause** because.

fer far.

288 **in his light**   in his way (preventing him from being noticed).
Notice the concentration of proverbs in this passage.

Alison and Nicholas Make their Plans:
Lines 289–310

In the carpenter's absence at Osney (again!), the lovers agree on a
plan to deceive him. After telling Alison to say that she does not
know where he is, Nicholas retires to his room with food and drink
for a couple of days. Obviously he does not expect the carpenter to
notice his absence for a while! Is this an agreed plan (293) or is
Nicholas in control (294)?

289 **ber thee wel**   conduct yourself well.
291 **bifel it**   it happened.
294 **Acorded been**   have agreed.
295 **shapen hym a wyle**   devise a stratagem, trick.
296 **sely**   simple, unfortunate. Does this word imply sympathy or
contempt?
   bigyle   deceive.
297 Does *game* mean scheme or does it tell us about their attitude?
   wente aright   worked, went according to plan.
301 **tarie**   remain, delay.
302 **dooth...carie**   makes someone carry. Even in small matters
Nicholas prefers that others should do the work.
   ful softe   very discreetly.
303 **mete**   food.
   tweye   two.
304 **bad**   told.
305 **axed**   asked.
306 **nyste**   (= *ne wiste*) did not know.
307 **ye**   eye.
308 **trowed**   thought, believed.
   maladye   sickness.
309 Because (*For*), in spite of (*for*) any cry her maid could make to
him.
310 **for...falle**   (in spite of) whatever might happen. Nicholas
thinks that Alison needs detailed instructions, but he is
confident that she will be able to trick John.

John Wonders what has Happened to Nicholas: Lines 311–39

Nicholas' plan begins to work. By Sunday evening John starts to wonder what has become of Nicholas, and sends his servant to find out. The servant cannot obtain an answer, but eventually, through a hole in the wall catches a glimpse of him staring upwards. He reports back to John. From 317–502, the tale switches predominantly into direct speech. How does Chaucer characterize John through the sounds and rhythms of his voice?

311   **passeth forth**   carries on.
       thilke   that same.
312   **stille**   quietly.
313   **hym leste**   pleased him.
314   Until sunset on Sunday.
315   **hath greet merveyle**   wondered greatly.
316   **Of**   about.
       eyle   ail, be wrong with.
317   **adrad**   afraid. Alison also swore by St Thomas (see line 183). These oaths may reflect Chaucer's knowledge of Oxford, since there was a church of St Thomas at Osney, or there may be a link with the Canterbury pilgrimage.
318   **It stondeth nat aright**   all is not well.
319   **shilde**   forbid.
320   **ful tikel**   very unstable. This banal phrase reveals the shallowness of John's thinking.
321   **saugh**   saw.
       cors yborn   body carried. What does John's amazement at this (presumably commonplace) event tell us about him?
322   **wirche**   work.
323   **knave**   servant.
325   **boldely**   immediately.
326   **sturdily**   resolutely, boldly.
328   **cride**   shouted. (Compare with Nicholas' plan [309].)
331   **noght**   nothing. Or at least he gave no sign of hearing.
332   He found (*foond*) a hole at the lower end of a plank (*bord*). The interior walls would have been wooden.
333   **Ther as**   where.

> **wont**   accustomed. Critics have commented on the amount of detail and explanation here.

334 **depe**   deeply. Does this mean he looked intently, or he looked in as far as he could see?

335 **hadde...sight**   caught a glimpse of him.

336 **evere capyng upright**   continually staring upwards.

337 **As he had kiked**   as if he had stared. Presumably he stares like a madman, and The Miller alludes to popular beliefs about the cause of lunacy.

338 **Adoun**   down.
   soone   at once.

339 **array**   condition.
   ilke   same.

John Responds to his Servant's Report: Lines 340–65

John attempts to come to terms with his sorrow at Nicholas' distress with a battery of proverbs and exemplary tales. Confident of the wisdom of ordinary people, he feels sure that Nicholas has over-reached himself and fallen into madness. But he also decides to take practical steps to bring him out of his trance. John's thoughts mix elements of wild surmise (343–4, 346), self-satisfaction (345, 347–8), half-appropriate anecdote (349–53), concern (354) and very physical forms of assistance (355–64). (See Approaches p. 101.)

340 **blessen hym**   cross himself.

341 St Frideswide (died around 735 AD) was supposed to have established a nunnery near Oxford. She became the patroness of the city. There was a parish church of St Frideswide which later became Christ Church Cathedral.

342 Little (*litel*) does a man know what will happen to him.

343 **is falle**   has fallen.
   astromye   astronomy. Does *with* imply that Nicholas has suffered 'as a result' of his astrological interests or 'in spite' of them (in that astrology might claim to give him some warning of catastrophe).

344 **woodnesse**   madness.

345 I always thought it would turn out like this.

346 **pryvetee** secrets (see Note to line 56, pp. 35–6). The intended irony here is that John is incapable of learning the lesson he teaches. Later in the poem he believes a secret about the future which turns out to be his undoing. There may also be an irony against The Miller, who in replying to The Reeve (56) used the same expression as the foolish carpenter uses here. (See Approaches, p. 121.)

347 **lewed** ignorant. What ironic point is made by John's praise of ignorance?

348 Who knows nothing apart from the Creed (*bileve*). The Creed is a statement of basic Christian beliefs which everyone was expected to know by heart.

349–52 This is a well-known story, versions of which can be found in Plato's *Theaetetus*, in Diogenes Laertius' *Lives of the Philosophers*, in *Aesop's Fables* and in Italian *novelle*. It may be a joke against the carpenter that he tells it as if it were personal experience because he is ignorant of its history.

349 **ferde** fared.

350–1 **prye...Upon** observe.

351 **what...bifalle** to find out from them what was going to happen.

352–3 Until he fell into a clay-pit (*marle-pit*). He had not foreseen that. This story is part of the struggle between the clever and the foolish which Nicholas began (191–2) and which ends only at the end of *The Miller's Tale*.

354 **Me reweth soore of** I am very sorry for.

355 **rated of** scolded for. In Middle English *studiyng* has its modern meaning of 'working to acquire learning', which is appropriate here, but it can also mean 'being in a state of mental perplexity', which may suit the sense of 'getting him out of his trance' implied in line 359.

357 **underspore** lever (the door) upwards from underneath. Robin, his servant, will raise the door enough for John to insert the staff which he will use as a lever to lift the door off its primitive hinges.

359 **gesse** imagine, suppose. For *studiyng* see Note to line 355, above.

360 **he gan hym dresse** he turned his attention to (or perhaps, he went to).

361 Compare with the description of The Miller, *General Prologue*, line 545, p. 1.

362 He heaved (*haaf*) it off by the fastenings (*haspe*) at once. The general meaning is clear enough but there is some doubt about the detail. If 'he' is John, then he heaves the door off its hinges (a possible meaning for *haspe*) and the door-opening goes according to plan. If 'he' is Robin then he grabs the door by the latch (which Nicholas has fastened on the inside) and he is so strong that he can pull the door off its hinges without a better hold.

John Rouses Nicholas from his Trance: Lines 366–92

Faced with Nicholas staring upwards, John employs both the means at his disposal: physical force (367–8) and popular religion which amounts almost to magic (369–78). Having put John into a state of alarm and wonder, Nicholas takes control of the situation, promising to tell John secret news after he has had a drink. How does John's use of charms (371–8) fit in with his earlier remarks about religious mysteries (346)?

366 **wende** thought. The medieval Christian was in danger of despair (*despeir*) either as a result of commerce with devils, or because of meditating on human sinfulness and the impossibility of meeting God's standards. John thinks Nicholas has fallen into despair. He responds by trying (not very competently) to exorcize any devils present (371) and by reminding Nicholas of God's forgiveness of sins as a consequence of Christ's suffering on the cross (370).

367 **hente** seized.

368 **spitously** loudly, vehemently.

369 John wants Nicholas to look down (*adoun*) to break the spell of whatever he is staring up at. But it would be more usual to tell people in despair to look up, to the cross or to the heavens.

370 **passioun** suffering (particularly applied to Christ's suffering on the cross on Good Friday).

371 I make the sign of the cross (*crouche*) to protect you from evil spirits (*elves*) and from wicked creatures (*wightes*). *Wight* usually means 'creature, person'. Possibly John uses it in an earlier more malevolent sense, or perhaps he misuses the word, thinking it has connotations of evil.

372 At that (*Therwith*) he said the night charm straightaway (*anon-rightes*). The night-charm (375–8) was a popular prayer, used by ordinary people as a protection against witchcraft.

373 **halves** sides. Presumably he makes the house safe by looking in each of the four directions in turn and then towards the threshold (*thresshfold* [374]) of the main doorway. Perhaps he recites the rhyme in each direction.

374 **withoute** outside. This would be the main entrance of the house.

375 St Benedict (*Benedight*), roughly 480–547, was the founder of the orders of monks (see Note to line 10, p. 31) in western Christianity.

377 The phrase *nyghtes verye* has been much argued over by critics and editors. Walter Skeat in *The Complete Works*, Vol V, p. 106, suggested that it might represent the oral survival of an Old English phrase *for nighte werigum* meaning *against the evil spirits of the night*. E. T. Donaldson in his essay, '*The Miller's Tale*', suggested that the scribes made a mistake, and that Chaucer wrote *nyghtes nerye*, which Donaldson glosses as *preserve us at night*.

Pater-noster is Latin for 'Our Father', the most famous of all Christian prayers. The *White Pater-noster* is a rhyme found in many European languages in several different versions, equivalent to:

Matthew, Mark, Luke and John
Bless the bed that I lie on.
Four corners to my bed,
Four angels round my head;
One to watch and one to pray
And two to bear my soul away.

(*The Oxford Dictionary of Nursery Rhymes*, ed. Iona and Peter Opie, pp. 303–05)

Perhaps John regards the text he recites *as the White Pater-noster* (Walter Skeat in *The Complete Works*, Vol V, p. 106 cites a variant which is almost a nonsense poem and which involves St Peter's brother), or perhaps his spell refers to the other rhyme for extra protection. This rhyme seems to lie on the border between a prayer (which is part of religion) and a magic spell (which is forbidden). In the Middle Ages, although some magical practices were certainly regarded as heathen, the border between magic and religion may have been fuzzy in places.

378 **wentestow** did you go. Probably St Peter's sister (about whom nothing is known) is here for the sake of the rhyme.

380 **Gan...soore** sighed deeply.

381 **eftsoones now** right now.

382 **seystow** do you say.

383 **swynke** labour, toil. John carries out his initial plan, seeking to combat what he sees as Nicholas' despair with simple piety.

384 **Fecche** fetch. Is Nicholas thirsty, or is there a psychological purpose?

385 **in pryvetee** privately, in confidence. (Compare with line 346 and see Approaches p. 122.)

386 **certeyn...toucheth** something that concerns.

387 **certeyn** for sure.

389 Because of the poor quality of drinking water, most English people drank beer to quench their thirst. Everyday beer consumed at all times of day was rather weak, but the *myghty ale* which John brings up himself (indicating the importance of the conversation?) was strong beer for serious drinking. A *quart* is an exact measure, two pints, a quarter of a gallon. Perhaps *large quart* implies a more approximate, generous amount, or it might refer to the large tankard which they share.

391 Nicholas locked (*faste shette*) the door again, but there is no reference to anyone putting it back on its hinges. This might mean that the door was easy to replace, or perhaps Chaucer forgot that the door had just been levered off.

392 And made the carpenter sit (*sette*) down beside him. Or *sette* may mean 'placed'.

Nicholas Tells John About the Second Flood: Lines 393–425

Nicholas begins the conversation by swearing John to secrecy with the threat of divine vengeance and madness. John defensively assures him that he is no tell-tale. This opens the way for Nicholas' revelation: as a result of his astrological speculations he has discovered that the world will be destroyed by a flood the following night. This news appals the carpenter, who is particularly troubled about what will happen to Alison. But Nicholas promises him that there is a way for the three of them to be saved. Why does John believe this story?

393 **hooste** landlord.

lief dear. Is Nicholas presenting himself to John as dependent (lodger), friend (*lief*), or superior (394–9)? (See Approaches, p. 122.)

394 **trouthe** troth, pledged word.

395 That you will not betray (*wreye*) this secret (*conseil*) to any man (*wight*).

397 **telle it man** tell it to anyone.

forlore utterly lost, damned.

398 **vengeaunce** punishment, revenge.

399 **be wood** go mad. Here John is threatened with madness if he betrays the secret. Later he is treated as mad because he believed it.

400 Christ's blood was an object of veneration in the Middle Ages because by shedding it Christ made possible the forgiveness of sins, and because wine was believed to turn into Christ's blood in the mass. So John's oath is a serious one.

401 **labbe** tell-tale, chatterbox.

402 Nor, though I say (*seye*) it myself do I enjoy talking too much (*gabbe*).

403 **wolt** wish.

404 **child ne wyf** anyone (literally, child nor woman). Christ harrowed (*harwed*) hell when, after his crucifixion, he went down to hell to free the righteous people from Old Testament times. The story appears only in the apocryphal (that is, 'not regarded as an authentic part of the *Bible*') *Gospel of Nicodemus*, but it was popular in the Middle Ages, perhaps because it shows Christ in a conventionally heroic role, rescuing prisoners from a castle. The story was dramatized in the English Mystery Plays and in *Piers Plowman*.

405-13 Notice how Nicholas' rhythms and sentence structures enable him to take control in this section.

406 **yfounde** found.

408 **a Monday** on Monday. Since they are speaking on Sunday evening the next Monday will be the following day.

at quarter nyght a quarter of the way through the night.

409 **wilde and wood**   strong and violent.

410 The story of the flood and Noah's (*Noes*) ark (from *Genesis*, 6–8) was a popular one in the Middle Ages, the subject of Mystery Plays and many types of visual depiction. That his flood should be like Noah's obviously appeals to John on religious grounds. But Nicholas' use of the comparison in deceiving him tells us about John's ignorance (in that God promised never again to destroy the world with water, *Genesis*, 9, 11–17) and his conceit (in that Noah was saved because he was the only virtuous man in the world). See Approaches p. 125.

411 The ludicrous speed with which the flood will cover the world makes John's credulity seem even more comic. In the *Bible* it rained for forty days.

412 **dreynt**   drowned, submerged.
   hidous   dreadful.
   shour   downpour.

413 **drenche**   drown.

417 **cas**   situation   (*cas* also has overtones of fate and destiny). Notice that John echoes what Nicholas said as he emerged from his trance (380–1).

419 **werken...reed**   act according to learning and advice.

420 **heed**   mind, thoughts.

421 **trewe**   wise.

422 **conseil**   advice.
   rewe   be sorry. The phrase occurs in the apocryphal book (see Note to line 404, p. 64) *Ecclesiasticus*, 32, 24, and in a work of Albertano of Brescia, where it is attributed to Solomon, and from where Chaucer took it. He also cites the phrase in *The Tale of Melibee* and *The Merchant's Tale*. Here Nicholas uses the authority of Solomon (*Salomon*) to browbeat John.

423 **wolt**   wish to.

424 **undertake**   promise.
   seyl   sail.

Nicholas Tells John how to Avoid the Flood: Lines 426–54

Nicholas takes advantage of John's rather dim recollection to retell the story of the flood, laying special stress on the difficulty Noah had in persuading his wife to enter the ark. His conclusion is that John must hurry to provide large vessels in which the three of them will be able to float and therefore avoid drowning. They will need food only for one day, since the flood is due to end within a few hours. Nicholas cleverly mixes story-telling with instructions to maintain his control over John. Why does he emphasize Noah's difficulties with his wife? How does he prevent John from trying to save the servants?

426 **Hastow nat**   have you not. In this passage Nicholas moves from rhetorical questions to commands.

   hou   how.

428 **lorn**   lost, destroyed.

429 **ful yoore ago**   a very long time ago.

430-5 This part of the story does not appear in the *Bible* but it formed a comic interlude in the Mystery Plays. Noah's wife is usually portrayed as a worldly, practical person who regards Noah's communing with God as daydreams, but is later forced to recognize the correctness of his actions.

431 **sorwe**   sorrow, trouble.

   felaweshipe   companions.

432 **Er**   before.

433 I dare well say that he would rather.

434 **thilke**   that.

435 Nicholas emphasizes the quarrel between Noah and his wife, rather than their subsequent reconciliation. Notice that he suggests that Noah might have preferred separate boats (an idea not found in other accounts).

436 **woostou**   do you know.

437 **asketh**   requires.

   hastif   urgent.

438 **tariying**   delay. Presumably preach (*preche*) is used in the sense of speaking at length.

439 **in**   house (especially lodging-house).

440 A kneading trough (*trogh*) was used for kneading dough. According to J. A. W. Bennett (*Chaucer at Oxford and Cambridge*, pp. 4–5), a kimlin (*kymelyn*) was a tray or trough used for baking or brewing. Both vessels needed to be large, fairly shallow and watertight.

442 **mowe**   may.

   swymme   float.

barge   boat, ship. In Middle English a *barge* is a sea-going vessel.

443   **vitaille**   victuals, food and drink.

suffisant   enough.

444   **fy on the remenant**   never mind the rest.

445   **aslake**   slacken, diminish, go down.

446   **pryme**   about nine o'clock in the morning.

447   **wite**   know.

448   **eek**   moreover. What is Nicholas' real reason for excluding Gill and Robin?

449   **Axe**   ask.

450   **pryvetee**   secrets.

451   Be satisfied unless you are going mad.

452   **greet**   great.

grace   mercy, forgiveness (especially God's forgiveness of sinners). This line makes explicit the greatness John is aspiring to. He will receive (and think himself worthy of) the same special grace as Noah.

453   **out of doute**   without doubt, without fear. Nicholas speaks of saving Alison, but he intends to sin with her.

454   **speed thee heer-aboute**   get on with this quickly.

More Advice from Nicholas and a Warning: Lines 455–92

Nicholas' directions become more detailed and more absurd. He even describes the conversation they will have once the boats are floating above the drowned streets of Oxford. Is all this detail primarily for the audience's amusement, or does it also play a part in the deception of John? Perhaps such persuasion involves selling someone a dream. In order to ensure their survival Nicholas insists that there must be silence in the three tubs, while they devote themselves to prayer (479), and that no sinful thoughts or looks must pass between John and his wife (482–3). Why does Nicholas emphasize the need for purity and religious devotion? What is his real reason for wanting John's tub far from Alison's? How do we react to him instructing John about sexual morality?

456   **Ygeten**   got, obtained.

457   The tubs could have been suspended in the attic above the upper bedrooms, but given that John later falls quite a long way into a place where his neighbours can come to see him, it is more likely that the tubs were suspended from the rafters of the hall, the main room in a medieval house, which was often two storeys high with the inside of the roof exposed.

458   **purveiaunce**   preparations, foresight.

460   **faire...yleyd**   properly stowed away in them.

461   **corde**   rope.
      atwo   in two, apart.

462   So that we can float free (*go*) when the water comes.

463   **an heigh**   high up, above. The *gable* is the part of the wall (here probably filled in with lath and plaster) which forms the vertical side for the sloping roof. They will float out over the stable (464) because it is only one storey high.

464   **gardyn-ward**   towards the garden.

466   Perhaps there is a contradiction here. The idea seems to be that the roof will protect them while it is raining, but when it stops (*goon away*) they will want to float out. But this implies that the flood will stop short of the second storey (since the water-level will not rise much after the rain stops) which would defeat the purpose of the flood. This may be a deliberate inconsistency alerting us to a weakness in Nicholas' plan (and to John's foolishness in believing him), or a real, if small, slip by Chaucer.

468   Nicholas evokes an image of marital harmony for John to dream of. This may relate back to the Mystery Play story of Noah, in which the wife becomes submissive after she enters the ark. But why does he envisage them as birds (compare with lines 126, 152, 174) and why is John compared to the female? (See Approaches p. 134.)

469   **clepe**   call.

473–4   Where before Nicholas tempts John with Noah's holiness, here he emphasizes his power. When everyone else is dead the three of them will be the rulers of the world.

475   **o**   one.
      ful right   very seriously.

476   **wel avysed**   very careful.

477   **shippes bord**   on board ship (that is, in their tubs).

479   Why does Nicholas insist that rather than calling out or lamenting they should be at prayer?

480 **heeste deere** precious command.

481 **moote...atwynne** must hang far apart.

482 The preaching of the Church took such a negative attitude to sexuality that even though (under the right circumstances) sex between married people was not regarded as sinful, John may well have thought that it was. Or perhaps the special circumstances of the second flood make it easier for Nicholas to convince John of the danger of sexual sin. There may also be an allusion to the tradition, believed by many early theologians and reported in medieval sermons, that there was no sexual activity in the ark. It may be worth remembering that on some interpretations the first flood was caused by sexual sin (*Genesis*, 6, 1–7).

483 **deede** action. Nicholas' reference to sinful glances and actions has been taken as an allusion to a passage from Jesus' 'Sermon on the Mount', *Matthew*, 5, 27-8:

> Ye have heard that it was said by them of old, Thou shalt not commit adultery; but I say unto you that whosoever looketh on a woman to lust after her hath committed adultery with her already in his heart.

Do you think this parallel helps Nicholas persuade John?

484 **ordinance is seyd** command has been given.

487 **abidyng...grace** awaiting the fulfilment of God's will.

488 **space** time.

489 *Sermonyng* means both 'preaching' and 'speaking at length'.

490 A proverb. If you send a wise man on an errand, you do not need to give detailed instructions. But he *has* given detailed instructions!

491 **it...teche** it is unnecessary to tell you what to do. Nicholas' plan should ensure that he and Alison can spend the night together, but what does he intend to do when the flood does not come?

John Prepares for the Flood: Lines 493–524

John tells Alison about the danger from the flood and begins to carry out Nicholas' instructions in order to save them all. The Miller pokes fun at John in several different ways: by calling him foolish (493), by telling us what Alison is really thinking (496), thus making her words (499–502) ironic, and by an exclamation in his own voice (503–5). Notice the preponderance of verbs as he describes John's frantic activity in carrying out Nicholas' strange orders (506–24).

494 **weylawey** alas.
495 John thinks the secret has become his, but it is no secret from Alison (496). She knows his private thoughts because Nicholas has told her what they will be. This transfer of secrets from the lovers to the husband parallels the transfer of Alison's *pryvetee* (see line 56) from John to Nicholas.
496 **war** aware.
     bet better.
497 **queynte cast** elaborate trick.
     seye mean.
498 **ferde as** acted as if.
     deye die.
500 **echon** all, each one.
501 **trewe, verray** faithful, true. Alison speaks about her fidelity while we know she is planning to be unfaithful. This might result in comic irony or it might undermine the meaning of the word 'truth'. (Compare with line 283.)
503-5 John's emotion (*affeccioun*) for Alison overwhelms his reason, in the same way that something may be so strongly present in someone's imagination (*ymaginacioun*) that they act (in the extreme case even dying) as if it were real. Is The Miller also implying that John has a strong imagination? What is the tone of voice here?
503 **which** what.
505 Such a deep impression (*impressioun*) may be recorded (within it). Medieval discussions of the workings of the mind often compared the trace of an object or concept in the memory and imagination to an impression made in wax.
506 **quake** tremble.
507 It seems to him that he can truly (*verraily*) see. He worries about the flood so powerfully and vividly that he thinks it is actually happening.
508 **walwynge** rolling, surging.
509 **drenchen** drown. Does John's anxiety prove the strength of his affection for Alison, or does it make him ridiculous?
510 **maketh sory cheere** looks miserable.

511 **sory swogh**   wretched groan.

514-15 Notice the further repetitions of *pryvely*, *pryvetee*, poking fun at John's belief in the secrecy of his actions, but also questioning the meaning of the word.

516 **His owene hand**   with his own hand. In order to avoid suspicion.

517 **stalkes**   uprights, as opposed to rungs (*ronges*).

518 **in the balkes**   among the, from the beams.

519 **hem vitailled**   provisioned them, stored food in them.

520 **jubbe**   jug.

521 **Suffisynge**   sufficient.

522 **array**   preparation.

523 **wenche**   womanservant.

524 **Upon his nede**   on his business. The journey to London would take at least two days in each direction.

John Awaits the Flood; Nicholas Takes Over his Bed: Lines 525–48

After a long day of preparation, John, Alison and Nicholas climb into their three tubs, say their prayers and wait for the flood. When John is asleep, Alison and Nicholas climb back down their ladders and go together to John's bed, where they make love until the early morning. The Miller emphasizes the pompous religiosity (530–4) and the exhaustion (535–9) of John the carpenter, and sets them against the discretion (540–2) and the pleasure (544–6) of the young couple. Do we feel sorry for John, or is it inevitable that Alison and Nicholas will enjoy each other in his bed while, lying in his tub, he dreams of salvation and power? What is the effect of the visual image (John in his tub among the rafters, the lovers in his bed below) which Chaucer and The Miller have created?

525 **whan it drow to nyght**   when it was nearly dark, at dusk.

526 Presumably candles were usually left burning, but John wants to give the impression that no one is ready to answer the door.

528 **clomben**   climbed.

529 **wel a furlong way**   a few minutes, at least the time it would take to walk a furlong (an eighth of a mile, just over 200 metres), which would be less than three minutes.

Notes

530 'Now say *The Lord's Prayer* and then be quiet (*clom*)', said Nicholas.
532 **devocioun** devotion, prayer.
533 **biddeth** prays, requests. Perhaps he repeats 'Our Father' and then adds another prayer of his own, or perhaps *devocioun* (532) indicates some longer sequence of prayers and praises which the carpenter (always?) says. Do you regard John as a religious person, or is he trying to live up to the role of Noah?
534 **it heere** might hear it.
535 **dede sleep** a very deep sleep.
for wery bisynesse because of the exertions of his activity, but the sense of 'wearied by his worries' may also be present.
537 **moore** later. Curfew time (*corfew-tyme*), the time of a bell which signalled that domestic fires should be covered and people return to their houses was about eight o'clock in the evening.
538 He groans deeply because of the suffering (*travaille*) of his spirit (*goost*).
539 **routeth** snores.
myslay was lying awkwardly. (See Approaches p. 128.)
540 **stalketh** creeps.
541 **ful...spedde** went down quickly and quietly.
543 **Ther as** where.
544 **revel** merriment.
545 **lith** lie.
546 Occupied (*In bisynesse*) with enjoyment (*mirthe*) and delight (*solas*).
547 **laudes** lauds, a church service which took place some time before dawn. Notice the different kinds of music here. (See Approaches pp. 128–9.)
gan to rynge began to ring.
548 **freres** friars. Only monks and friars would have to attend lauds.
chauncel chancel, area of the church in front of the main altar.

Absolon Decides to Speak to Alison at her Window: Lines 549–78

Absolon concludes that John has gone on a business trip and decides to take advantage of his absence by making another visit to Alison's bedroom window, to confess his love to her and, he hopes, to receive a kiss in return. We learn about the way Absolon has been watching John's door (565–6), and enquiring of the monks about his whereabouts (553–62). But Absolon is also a practical lover. His suffering for love (550) does not prevent him from enjoying the company of his friends (552). He decides to stay awake all night like a lover (564) but goes home to sleep first (577). We also learn more about John's working habits, his absences from home, and the trust the Abbey places in his judgement (557–60). What is the effect of giving this information at this point?

552 **hym to disporte**   to enjoy himself.

553 **upon cas**   by chance.

     cloisterer   monk (one of the monks of Osney Abbey, presumably).

554 **after**   about.

555 **drough hym apart**   took him aside. Again the emphasis is on secrecy. Presumably Absolon and his friends went into the Abbey church, where Absolon happened to meet a monk he knew who took him outside to answer his question. As with the lauds bell (547), and the pilgrimage itself, there is an interesting mingling and separation of secular pleasure and religious observance around the church. Absolon finds his informant inside the church and asks the leading question there, but the monk prefers to answer privately outside.

556 **noot**   (= *ne woot*) do not know.

557 **Syn**   since. The implication is that John has work to do at the Abbey almost every day.

     trowe   think, believe.

558 **ther**   wherever. It would be usual for someone responsible for a large building to send a carpenter to a wood (which might be at some distance and might belong to the Abbey) to select timber for repairs or additions. While they were away they would stay at the *grange* (560), a farm building or granary which would be part of the Abbey estate.

561 The monk tells Nicholas that John must either be away or at his own house. Since Nicholas has not seen John at home, he reasons that he must be away, even though his informant said he had no certain knowledge (562).

562 **soothly**   truly.

563 **joly**   lively, sprightly (this adjective is often used of Absolon).

light   cheerful, glad.

565 **stirynge**   moving.

566 **sprynge**   break.

567 **So moot I thryve**   As I may prosper (a common exclamation).

568 How do you understand *pryvely* here? (Compare with other references to secrecy in lines 554, 514 and 56.)

569 Which stands low down on his bedroom wall (*boures wal*).

571 **I shal nat mysse**   I shall not fail.

572 **leeste**   least.

573 **parfay**   by my faith (a common light exclamation).

574 **icched**   itched. Is this ironic in view of line 626?

576 **me mette**   I dreamed (presumably this was on Sunday night).
   feeste   feast. Perhaps this is an ironic reference back to the lovers' *revel* (544).

577 If Absolon has an early evening nap he will be better able to stay up all night. But how does this practicality place Absolon in relation to the love convention he is trying to follow? Noble lovers stay up all night because they are too anxious to sleep. Absolon sleeps much longer than he intends (579).

578 **pleye**   frolic, amuse myself (the word also has a sexual sense which may be ironic here, since as Absolon sleeps Nicholas and Alison *pleye*).

Absolon Goes to the Window and Confesses his Love: Lines 579–605

Just before dawn, much later than he intended, Absolon wakes up and prepares himself to address Alison. When he speaks to her in the elaborate language of the lover, she tells him plainly that she has another lover, and that he should go away and let her sleep. Absolon prepares thoroughly, taking particular care that his breath should smell sweet (582–5). He hopes that the kiss he has set his heart on will be the first of many, and he wants Alison to enjoy it. Is this considerate or ridiculous? His language (which may refer to *The Song of Solomon*, a book of the *Bible*, which describes God's love of the Church in the form of a love-poem) evokes the sweet herbs he has chewed (590-91) and the animal imagery (591, 596–8) associated with Alison earlier (126, 150–5, 174). Does the language suit his station and emotions? (See Approaches p. 128.) What do you make of the contrast with the language of her reply (600–05)?

579 Presumably (see line 623) the first cock crows some time before dawn. But still Absolon has slept most of the night, whereas Nicholas and Alison, who were making love until lauds, have been asleep only for an hour or two. Perhaps this suggests a contrast between the (theoretical) wakefulness of the courtly lover and the more practical wakefulness of Nicholas, the successful lover. (Compare also with lines 247–9.)

580 **rist** rose.

581 And dresses himself (*arraieth*) handsomely (*gay*) to the last detail (*poynt-devys*).

582 **greyn** cardomom seed, a hot sweet-smelling spice. Nicholas' natural sweetness is compared to liquorish (99).

584 **trewe-love** herb paris (called a true love because the shape of its four leaves resembles a love-knot), carried (*beer*) for the smell (or perhaps for the name).

585 **gracious** pleasing, attractive.

586 **rometh** makes his way (perhaps an ironic use of a courtly word).

588 **Unto...raughte** it reached only up to his chest. Or perhaps a little below, since when Absolon kneels his face is level with the window (615).

589 **semy soun** small or soft sound.

590 **What do ye** How are you? Absolon uses the submissive, polite pronoun.

590-1 Honey-comb (*hony-comb*) and cinnamon (*cynamome*) are both terms of affection found in *The Song of Solomon*, 4, 11 and 14.

591 **bryd** bird. Absolon uses the vocabulary of popular lovesongs.

592 **Awaketh** wake up (imperative form).

593 **Wel litel** very little.

594 **I swete ther I go** I sweat wherever I go. Absolon interprets it as a sign of love, but Alison may find this characteristic off-putting.

595 It is no wonder if I melt (*swelte*) and sweat.

596 **moorne** mourn.
    tete teat.

598 **turtel** turtle-dove.

599 Absolon means to say that his appetite is much reduced because

of love (which would be a typical symptom of courtly love), but he ends up saying that he eats the same as a young girl.

600 **Go fro**   go away from. Presumably Jack fool is an expression of contempt.

601 **"com pa me"**   come kiss me (possibly the words were from a popular song).

602 Would she be at fault (*to blame*) if she did not have another lover whom she loved better than Absolon? Or is she pretending to refer to her husband?

604 What does this threat tell us about her opinion of Absolon?

605 **a twenty devel wey**   in the name of twenty devils.

Alison Puts her Bottom out of the Window: Lines 606–35

Absolon agrees to go away in return for a kiss. For her amusement and Nicholas', Alison puts her bottom out of the window. When Absolon kisses what he takes to be her face, he is at first surprised at her beard, but then realizes the mistake he has made, to much laughter from the lovers. This is the first climax of the story, and it is worth observing how Chaucer keeps in play the separate voices (and outlooks) of his three characters alongside his narrative voice and the dominating visual image of the would-be lover kneeling in the dark and kissing whatever emerges from the window. In the other versions of this story which we have (and which we presume Chaucer worked from) it is the successful male lover who bares his bottom. What are the advantages (for the story) of Alison conceiving and carrying out this insulting joke? Do you think Absolon deserves to have this trick played on him? (See Approaches pp. 115–16.)

607 **so yvel biset**   so badly misplaced (or possibly, so badly mistreated). Absolon continues to flatter himself that he is a true lover.

608 **syn...bet**   since it cannot turn out any better .

610 **Wiltow**   (= *wilt thow*) will you.

611 **certes**   certainly.

614 **hust**   hush, be quiet. Alison's action could be interpreted mainly as a lesson for Absolon or mainly as a joke to be shared

with Nicholas. How does this relate to the idea of sharing secrets/*pryvetee* in the tale? (It is worth noting that some good early manuscripts omit lines 613–14, but most editors think Chaucer wrote them.)

615 **doun sette hym** got down. He has to do this because the window is so low (if the window were higher Alison's trick would not work), but it adds to the humorous visual symbolism (the courtly lover on his knees to his mistress), and to his humiliation, that Absolon should be kneeling.

616 **at alle degrees** in every way (perhaps, at every stage). In either case Absolon thinks he is managing his affair successfully, imagining that what Alison sees as a goodbye kiss will actually be the first of many (617).

618 Sweetheart, give me your favour (*grace*) and sweet bird, your mercy (*oore*).

619 **undoth** undoes, opens.

620 'Have done', she said, 'hurry up, and be quick.' Hurrying him seems to be a way of dominating Absolon. This is one of Nicholas' techniques.

622 **gan wype** wiped.

623 **pich** pitch.

624 Is it the rhyme or the word order that makes this line so funny?

625 **hym...wers** nothing better or worse happened to him (that is, exactly this happened).

626 **But** than.
    ers arse. The very coarse vocabulary of the narration reflects the actions here and contrasts with Absolon's language.

627 **Ful savourly** with relish, carefully registering the taste and smell.

628 **Abak he stirte** he started, or jumped, back. When Chaucer writes 'he thought there was something wrong', is this comic understatement or are we watching Absolon's (rather slow) mind in action?

629 **wiste** knew. How does mentioning the beard increase the humour?

630 **long yherd** long-haired.

631 *Fy* and *allas* are both exclamations, but the sequence is important. Absolon feels contempt and anger, and then sorrow (for himself).
    do done.

632 **clapte** slammed. How does *Tehee* add to our sense of Alison's personality?

633 **a sory pas** with sad steps. Is Absolon wiser now?

634 Some critics see a pun here: the first beard is literal, the second a metaphorical sense meaning 'joke'. It may be a problem that Nicholas has to overhear Absolon's thought about Alison's 'beard'. What does *hende* mean here (see Note to line 91, p. 41)?

635 **corpus** (Latin) body.
faire and weel marvellously. Does Nicholas appreciate Alison better now?

Absolon Learns his Lesson and Plans his Revenge: Lines 636–77

As Absolon hears the mocking laughter of Alison and Nicholas he realizes the depth of his humiliation. Anger and disgust give way to thoughts of revenge. He walks across the street to a blacksmith's forge and borrows a red hot plough-blade. The passage contrasts the physicality of Absolon's attempts to clean his mouth (639–40) with his mental anguish (641–51), the labour of the smithy (654–5) with the realistic social exchange (656–76). Absolon may be humiliated in the semi-private world of the love triangle but he has a network of acquaintances who are more than ready to exchange favours with him.

636 **sely** hapless, unfortunate.
every deel every part, every word.

637 To bite one's lip was a conventional indication of anger in Middle English. There may also be special reasons why Absolon bit his.

638 Why do you think Absolon switches to the intimate pronoun (*thee*) now? (Compare with line 590 and see A Note on Chaucer's English, p. 147.)

639 **froteth** rubs, chafes. The sentence is a rhetorical question: who now rubs his mouth but Absolon?

640 **sond** sand.
chippes woodchips. (See Approaches, p. 131.)

642 May I give my soul to Satan. The sentence is conditional. May I give my soul to Satan if I would not rather be avenged than...

643-4 If I would not rather (*levere*) be avenged (*awroken*) for this insult (*despit*) than own this whole town, he said.

645 What a pity that I did not avoid (*ybleynt*) it.

646 **yqueynt** quenched.

648 He did not consider love (*paramours*) worth anything, (*kers* means cress).

649 Is he cured of love or of the sickness of seeing himself and others in a false light?

650 **gan deffie** denounced. Not only has he finished with love himself, but he tries to warn others against it. Perhaps Absolon continues to make himself ridiculous.

651 **weep** wept.

652 **A softe paas he wente** he walked quietly (or perhaps slowly). What is the significance of Absolon's quiet calmness here and later (656)?

653 To (*Until*) a blacksmith whom people called master Gervase. Blacksmiths did virtually all metalwork as well as shoeing horses. Their shops would be at work early in the morning, making, sharpening and repairing implements required for the day's work. (For the realism of the forge, see Approaches p. 94.)

654 **smythed** made, or repaired.
plough harneys ploughing gear.

655 **sharpeth** sharpens. The Miller mentions metal parts of the plough. The coulter (*kultour*) is an iron blade which cuts the earth vertically. It is placed in front of the share (*shaar*) which horizontally splits apart the earth above the coulter and lifts it to the side.

659 **for Cristes sweete tree** by Christ's blessed cross.

660 **rathe** early.
benedicitee bless me.

661 **gay gerl** amorous girl (perhaps with an implication of immorality). Like Absolon, Gervase associates early mornings with love.

662 This is the only known occurrence of the word *viritoot* and no one really knows what it means. The most common explanation is 'on the move' or 'astir'. But perhaps it should be part of Gervase's rude banter, possibly as a colloquial expression which was never otherwise recorded in a written source.

663 St Neot (*Note*) was an Anglo-Saxon saint of the Ninth century, about whom very little is known. There are legends associating him with Oxford.

664 **ne roghte nat a bene**   did not care a bean.

665 **no word agayn he yaf**   he did not say a word in reply.

666 **tow**   flax. A distaff (*distaf*) is an implement used in spinning thread. But this expression is a proverb meaning 'to have business in hand'.

668 **chymenee**   fireplace, hearth.

669 Lend it me; I have something to do with it.

670 **agayn**   back.

672 **poke**   bag.

nobles alle untold   uncounted, countless gold coins (compare with line 148).

673 **Thou sholdest have**   you should have it. His conversations with Gervase show us another side to Absolon's character, placing his former courtly pretensions in a context of ordinary working life.

674 **Ey, Cristes foo!**   By the Devil.

675 **be as be may**   be that as it may. For the present Absolon will give no explanations.

676 **to-morwe day**   another time.

677 **caughte**   picked up.

stele   handle.

Absolon's Revenge: Lines 678–705

With the plough-coulter in hand, Absolon goes to the window and begs another kiss, offering Alison a gold ring if she agrees. To complete the joke Nicholas puts his bottom out of the window and lets fly a fart. But his joke turns against him in the second climax of the story. Instead of a kiss he receives the red-hot coulter which burns the skin all around his bottom. Each character in this passage aims to mislead the person they address and is in turn misled by the reply. But the comedy of misunderstanding turns physical with Nicholas' fart and Absolon's hot knife. Even the latter is misdirected, since Absolon intends to take revenge on Alison. (See Approaches pp. 114–20.)

678 **gan to stele**   crept out.

683 **warante**   swear, wager.

684 **leef**   beloved (see line 285). Absolon's language and his offer seem very suspicious. Why do the lovers not suspect his plan?

687 **yaf**   gave.

688 **therto wel ygrave**   also beautifully engraved.

689 **yeve**   give. Absolon uses polite thou-forms to stress his humility.

690 **was risen**   had got up.

691 **amended al the jape**   improve the joke. Nicholas may make his extraordinary mistake because he now has complete contempt for Absolon, or because he is trying to compete with Alison.

693 Presumably the window is hinged at the top.

694 How does *pryvely* function here?

695 **Over**   beyond.

696 **therwith**   at that. At the second climax of the poem Chaucer reminds us that both Absolon and Nicholas are clerks.

697 **I noot nat**   I do not know. This sentence combines love-flattery with practicality: Absolon needs a sound to aim at. Why does Alison not answer? Does she see through his trick?

698 **leet fle**   let fly.

699 **thonder-dent**   thunderclap. Perhaps we should remember Nicholas' storm.

700 **yblent**   blinded.

701 **iren hoot**   hot iron implement.

702 **smoot**   struck.

703 **Of**   off.
   an hande-brede about   a hand's breadth around.

704 **toute**   buttocks.

705 **smert**   pain. In what ways is this extremely painful punishment appropriate for Nicholas?

John's Fall and the Reaction of his Neighbours: Lines 706–46

Nicholas shouts for water to treat his burns. His cries wake John who, thinking that the flood has come, cuts his tub loose from the rafters. He falls straight to the floor and knocks himself out. Alison and Nicholas run out into the street shouting, at which the neighbours come in and stare at John. The lovers' version of events is accepted by the town and he is ridiculed as a madman. The Miller ends by listing the penalties paid by the three men.

What does Chaucer do to keep his third climax a surprise? It is possible to see the way the three stories (the flood, the kiss, the branding) interact as humorous coincidence, but it may be an example of the way in which a greater design can operate through the stratagems and mistakes of individual characters. Should we regard this as God's plan working in the world, or is it at best 'poetic justice'?

Why are John's neighbours introduced at the end of the tale? Perhaps there is a connection between the way Nicholas uses the story of the flood to trick John (405–54) and the way he successfully rewrites the tale to his own advantage at the end (716–41). We may feel sympathy for John as the victim of Nicholas' imagination and reinterpretation.

707 **herte** heart. The sacred heart (of Jesus) was an object of veneration in the Middle Ages, but in Nicholas' state any oath will do.

708 **sterte** awoke, leaped.

709 **oon** someone.

710 *Nowelis* is John's dim recollection of Noah's name (compare with line 429), with a little help from Christmas.

711 **He sit hym** he sat. Is it significant for the rest of the tale that John says no more (*mo*) words here?

713 **foond** tried.
selle sell. The general meaning is that he fell directly to the ground, without having time to do anything. Editors usually explain Chaucer's use of this phrase by referring to a similar phrase ('and while he was falling he did not find any bread to sell') in *Aloul*, an Old French *fabliau*. Bread and ale were already in the tub. This may be the best we can do, but I wish there was something better, especially in view of the awkward repetition in lines 714–15.

714 **celle** floor.

715 **aswowne** in a faint, unconscious.

716 **stirte hire** jumped. While John is unconscious the two lovers ensure that their version of events is heard first. Nicholas is already out of bed.

718 **smale and grete**   poor and rich (that is, everyone).

719 **In ronnen**   run in.

   gauren on   stare at.

720 *Wan* is another word for pale.

721 **brosten**   broken. What would breaking his arm mean to John the carpenter?

722 Do you take *stonde* (stand) literally ('he must get up') or metaphorically ('he must take responsibility' or 'he must face up to')?

   unto   to, for, in spite of (depending on how *stonde* is understood).

723 **bore doun**   overcome, contradicted.

724 **With**   by. Is *hende* simply sarcastic here?

726 **agast so**   so afraid. (For *Nowelis* see Note to line 710, p. 82.) Apparently they overhear John's thought.

727 **fantasie**   imagination (or perhaps, delusion). Which seems better to you? It would make sense to have a comma after *fantasie*.

   vanytee   foolishness. How do Alison's and Nicholas' choice of words distort the story we have heard? Can you think of fairer words?

728 **yboght hym**   bought himself.

731 *par compaignye*   to keep him company. How does the use of a French phrase here, and the reference to God (730), add to the sense of ridicule? Compare the other uses of *compaignye* in the tale (96, 552).

732 **fantasye**   delusion.

733 Notice how the people now stare in amazement at John's actions using the same words with which Nicholas tricked him at 335–6.

734 Compare with line 282, where all Absolon's *ernest* is made into a joke. In defending his choice of tale The Miller upheld the related proposition that jokes should not be taken seriously (78). This interest in the exchanges between jest and *ernest* is very characteristic of Chaucer. Might we take this line as inviting some sympathy for John?

735 **what so**   whatever.

736 **reson**   reason(s), explanations. A very strong way of expressing the frustration of John's situation. What is the state of John's reason if no one pays attention to his version of events? But his experience

of failing to make sense corresponds to something real in the tale. There seems to be a rational explanation given for everything which happens, yet so much of it is weird and fantastical.

737 **sworn adoun** overcome (or silenced) by what they swore to. Compare with the Modern English phrase 'shouted down'. What does it mean that John is overcome by their strong oaths (*othes grete*) rather than their reasons?

738 **holde wood** considered mad. Why *holde*? Why might being treated as a madman by his neighbours be a suitable punishment for John? (Compare with line 452.)

739 For all the men of learning immediately sided with their fellow. Here *clerk* must refer to the teachers (and perhaps the priests) as well as the students. This line increases our feeling that people are conspiring against John.

741 **stryf** quarrel, commotion.

742 Polite editors (the majority) gloss *swyved* as 'copulated with', but 'screwed' gives a better idea of the tone. Notice that the verb is in the passive here. Is this part of John's public humiliation or something that only the lovers know? Which of the three penalties paid by John (being cuckolded, breaking his arm, being treated as a madman) would be most painful to him?

743 **For al his kepyng** in spite of all his guarding.

744 **nether ye** anus (literally, lower eye).

746 Is The Miller's blessing affected by the line it rhymes with?

The Reeve's Prologue

Reaction to *The Miller's Tale*

The main purpose of *The Reeve's Prologue* is to introduce *The Reeve's Tale* by presenting The Reeve's intention and preoccupations. But we also learn how the pilgrims in general, and The Reeve in particular, reacted to *The Miller's Tale*. We are told that many of them laughed (747), that different people reacted differently (749), that most of them took it light-heartedly (750), and that only The Reeve was really upset. How does this compare with the reaction to *The Knight's Tale* (1–5)? Might you have expected more reaction?

The Reeve's intervention in *The Miller's Prologue* (36–41) has already prepared us for his angry response. Now he explains that he resents the slur against carpenters (753, 806), that he would like revenge (756, 803-08), and that he is old (759). Is The Reeve's description of the vices of old men (760-90) a reason for not taking revenge (759), a fragment of autobiography, or an explanation of the depth of his feelings? Do you think it reasonable that The Reeve should regard *The Miller's Tale* as a personal attack on him?

747 **nyce** foolish.

751 **hym greve** become angry.

754–5 *Litel* and *lite* may be ironic understatement.

755 **gan to grucche** complained.

756 **So theek** (= *so thee ik*) as I may prosper.

757 **bleryng...ye** (a tale of) deceiving a proud miller, literally dimming his eye.

759 **me...age** I do not wish to joke because of my age. Or perhaps he means that he has no wish to tell a tale, but he seems keen enough later.

760 The Reeve imagines himself as an old horse, who no longer eats grass in the field, but whose only food (*fodder*) is dry winter food (*forage*) in the stable.

761 **writeth** declares, signifies.

762 **mowled** gone mouldy. His white hairs (*white top*) are now envisaged as fibres of mould growing out of his head.

763 The fruit of the medlar tree was called an open-arse (*open-ers*) on account of its appearance, and was usually eaten when it was almost rotten.

765 **mullok** rubbish.
stree straw.

768 **hoppen** dance.
pype play a tune.

769 **wyl** will, wishes (with a strong sexual overtone, brought out in line 770).
ther...nayl one desire always remains, sharp as a nail.

770 **hoor** grey-haired.
grene tayl youthful, vigorous sexual organ.

772 **evere in oon** continually.

773 How do you reconcile this line with his earlier remark that age would prevent him from engaging in a contest of ribaldry

(758–9)? Might it be that he takes a grimmer, less amused view of sexual desire than The Miller?

774 **asshen olde** old ashes.

yreke covered over (but still present).

775 **gleedes** glowing coals. In making this division of vices The Reeve imitates the methods of medieval preachers.

776 **Avauntyng** boasting.

coveitise covetousness, strong desire for possessions, especially (but not only) those belonging to other people.

777 **longen** belong.

eelde old age.

778 **lemes** limbs.

unweelde feeble, unwieldy.

780 **a coltes tooth** the desires of a young man. This is a proverbial expression, but notice that The Reeve again uses an image connected to horses.

781 **henne** hence, away.

782–7 The Reeve employs an extended metaphor from the handling of wine-barrels. The tap *tappe* was a thick tapered stick pushed into the tap-hole (also known as the tap as in line 785) to close the barrel (*tonne* [786]), and removed to allow the wine to flow out. The barrel was placed on its side, so that when it was first opened the wine poured out vigorously. Later on, the flow reduced to a trickle, when the wine might drip onto the rim (*chymbe* [787]) of the barrel. The Reeve compares this gradual loss of vigour to his experience of life, and particularly to his sexual capability. The idea that decay is implicit even in youth is brought out by the image of Death (*Deeth* [784]) as the tapster who first pulled out the tap (*drough the tappe* [784]) when The Reeve was born (*bore* [783]).

788 **chymbe** chime.

789 **ful yoore** long ago.

790 Old people have nothing left except the folly of age (*dotage*).

793 **amounteth** amount to.

794 **hooly writ** scripture.

796 **soutere** cobbler.

leche doctor.

798 **Lo Depeford** Here is Deptford (then a village about 6 km from Southwark).

half-wey pryme about 6.30 am.

799 **Grenewych** Greenwich (about 1 km further on their journey). Probably Chaucer was living there in the 1390s. The reference to rogues (*many a shrewe*) should be taken as a self-deprecating joke.

803 **sette his howve** tip his hood, make him look a fool.

804 It is allowed (*leveful*) to repel (*of-showve*) force with force.

807 **Peraventure** perhaps.

809 **cherles termes** rude words.

810 **to-breke** be broken apart.

812 **balke** beam. The Reeve is alluding to the sermon on the mount, where Jesus castigates hypocrites who can detect small faults in others but are blind to much larger faults in themselves. (See *Matthew*, 7, 3.)

Approaches

Approaches through Sources and Influences

The Miller's Prologue

In the *General Prologue*, Chaucer offers an apology: he will have to tell the tales using the language in which they have originally been told, and this may offend. He presents this apology at length, and as if to reinforce his point, he mentions two authoritative examples of great men who spoke in a plain way: Christ, and the Greek philosopher, Plato (see *General Prologue* lines 725–746). This apology may not be entirely genuine.

In order to help us understand Chaucer's position, we need to distinguish between the roles that Chaucer assumes for himself in the poem. There is one voice for Chaucer himself, Chaucer the Poet; there is another for Chaucer the Pilgrim. Think of the poet as the writer, the person who constructs the entire work; think of the pilgrim as the created character behind the various statements and points of view that are given. This is the person who intrudes, using 'I' or 'Me', or as the man who speaks directly to the reader, for example:

> My wit is short, ye may wel understonde.
> (*General Prologue* [746])

> Blameth nat me if that ye chese amys.   (73)

In both the *General Prologue* and *The Miller's Prologue*, he may be making it easier for himself to tell stories which are likely to offend. Chaucer, as poet, relishes the prospect of telling an entertaining bawdy tale, but his pilgrim character holds reservations:

> Avyseth yow, and put me out of blame;   (77)

These reservations add to the humour. It is as if the poet has planted a character in among the other pilgrims on these occasions to express a false sense of reservation and decorum. The effect may be that the reader anticipates all the more keenly the bawdy stories!

Remember that all the stories belong to the pilgrims – they are, apparently, told by the pilgrims. But they are, from another perspective, Chaucer's own stories. One quite clever feature is the way that Chaucer matches his tales to the tellers, and the first tale, The Knight's is usually interpreted as a noble and heroic story set in Ancient Greece. The story derives from a tale by the Italian poet, Boccaccio. It is a story entirely in keeping with The Knight's personality (honourable, noble) and by general agreement, it gets the story-telling competition off to a good start:

> In al the route nas ther yong ne oold
> That he ne seyde it was a noble storie   (2–3)

The Host, delighted that his game of story-telling has been *wel bigonne* (9) assumes that the next tale will be of similar noble content and theme, and that it will naturally be told by The Monk, he being next in line of social importance. Accordingly, The Monk is asked to find a story *to quite with the Knyghtes tale* (11) – to match The Knight's. Then, all of a sudden, The Miller insists on telling his tale, and, using an arrogant and assertive tone, it is clear that he intends to get his way.

As is the case with many other tales in the collection we can detect a link between tale and teller. To begin to understand this relationship you need to refer again to the description of The Miller from the *General Prologue*, (see p.1). He is a larger-than-life character who loves buffoonery and indecent stories. He is unscrupulous, dishonest in temperament and brawny of appearance. These characteristics appear to be developed through his intimidating and overpowering behaviour in *The Miller's Prologue* when he rides roughshod over all other views and insists on the right to tell his story. You will find more connections between the character and his story in the tale itself – the *General Prologue* informs us that he loves lewd stories, and when we read his own tale, we are not disappointed.

Activity

Look carefully at the words exchanged between The Miller and The Host (20–35) and those between The Miller and The Reeve (36–58). What impressions do you gain of the character of The Miller? Re-read the portrait of The Miller in the *General Prologue*. Can you see how characteristics of The Miller are further developed in *The Miller's Prologue*? Then look at what Chaucer himself has to say from line 59. What is *his* role in *The Miller's Prologue*?

Discussion

In the *General Prologue* we learnt that The Miller could break doors off their hinges or charge them down with his head. Now we learn that he is drunk. As well as sitting precariously on his horse, he speaks *in Pilates voys* (16), and admits to his own inebriation:

'But first I make a protestacioun
That I am dronke; I knowe it by my soun.   (29–30)

and, perhaps most significantly, he insists on making his point: *For I wol speke or elles go my wey* (25). The Host is moved to warn that, in his opinion, The Miller's *wit is overcome* (27).

The Miller is going to tell a bawdy story about the 'cuckolding' of a husband, much of the content of which, and certainly the tone, will contrast with *The Knight's Tale*. Although this might seem out of place here, it was not an uncommon sort of theme. It is clear that, far from feeling uneasy about it, Chaucer wanted to include such a story.

In the Old French poem, the *Roman de la Rose* there were passages about jealous husbands having to be on their guard to avoid being made fools by their wives. The Reeve insists that it is sinful to defame husbands and talk about women doing such dreadful things, and concludes that The Miller could find plenty of better ideas for a tale:

'Thou mayst ynogh of othere thynges seyn.'   (41)

What of Chaucer's role in *The Miller's Prologue*? Notice that he, somewhat characteristically, stands back from the conversations between The Host, The Reeve and The Miller. The Miller insists on going ahead with his tale, and in spite of his drunken state, his reasons are quite clearly expressed and they even seem convincing. Why, he asks, is there any need for offence?

Do you detect possible contradictions in The Miller's reply at this point? He dismisses the objections; just because he has a tale to tell about a jealous husband, he says that does not mean to say that he, or The Reeve, or anybody else, is tarred by the same brush. But, in spite of his drunkenness (or perhaps because of it) his speech here is full of double sexual meanings, particularly centred on the the word *pryvetee* (56), meaning both 'secrets' and 'private parts' or 'genitals'. (See Notes pp. 35–6.) Those pilgrims with their wits about them will have realized that this apparent justification for his tale may simply have been another means of whetting their appetites for the outrageous sexual behaviour that is about to follow in the tale. Another interpretation of The Miller's speech here, also connected with the sexual pun, is the view that so long as a husband gets what he wants from his wife, he should not go looking too closely into her private life.

Having listened to The Miller's conversations with The Host and The Reeve, Chaucer is, somewhat wrily, lost for words, or he appears to be: *What sholde I moore seyn...* (59). He might deliberately be taking this position. Can you see the position that Chaucer has cleverly got himself into? Very soon after the initial apology that he made in the *General Prologue*, and following just one honourable tale of nobility, (The Knight's), offensive language will now have to be used to tell a tale that The Host has agreed to. And the reader will hardly wish to miss this prospect. Consider the last section of *The Miller's Prologue*, (59–78); we are told that if we do not like the language we are about to hear, then we must: *Turne over the leef and chese another tale;* (69).

My reaction is to do the opposite! Chaucer has tempted his readers to read on, he has revealed quite a lot more of The Miller's character, but above all he has been able to disclaim responsibility for the sort of language that is going to be spoken, blaming it instead on The Miller.

The next section, on *fabliau,* helps you to understand the literary significance of Chaucer's choice for this, his second story.

Fabliau

Chaucer prepares the ground for the telling of a bawdy tale in *The Miller's Prologue*. As he has explained, he will need to employ language which is earthy and crude and which tells of events which themselves are down-to-earth and crude. Derek Pearsall, in *The Canterbury Tales*, p. 173, suggests that one reason for choosing *fabliau* as a genre is that Chaucer was able to reflect in the tale the reality of experience in life. Although courtly romance, as it appeared in *The Knight's Tale*, could reflect certain aspects of life, the *fabliau* could help him to create a more realistic story, dealing with experience in a different way. Noble and heroic actions in many a courtly romance would have presented love as idealistic and serious; *fabliaux* would have dwelt more on the comic and realistic events in the affairs of love. Many *fabliaux* were in fact erotic by nature.

Chaucer borrowed from the French and Flemish traditions of *fabliau,* and developed many new features of his own. The original features of *fabliau* are summarized in the Notes on pp. 38–9 and other examples of *fabliaux* can be found in the Appendix pp.166–7. When you begin to think about what Chaucer added to the basic elements of bawdiness, crude humour, parody and stock characters, you may realize that he was a master of adaptation. As is suggested in the Notes p. 38, the hilarious vulgarity of the *fabliau* is evident in the poem, but it is obviously more than just a bawdy romp.

Activity

This activity involves studying the Notes pp. 38–9, introducing the genre of *fabliau,* and reading the two examples of other *fabliaux* in the Appendix pp. 166–7. Make a list of the features in *The Miller's Tale* which make up the basic *fabliau* genre. What has Chaucer added to the basic French and Flemish forms of *fabliau*? Give examples from the text of these new features. Look at the events, the characters and the language.

Discussion

Chaucer added a lot more realism and also developed description and characterization. He also imposed cruel ironies on the characters in his *fabliaux* tales.

An interesting idea, suggested by the critic D. S. Brewer in his essay, 'The *Fabliaux*' (see Rowland, ed. 1968), is that Chaucer's *fabliaux* tales are marked out by their mixture of styles: courtly and romantic on the one hand, realistic or naturalistic, on the other. As well as a move towards naturalism, *The Miller's Tale* can be seen as a work with powerful religious ironies and structures. Its framework of basic temptations or sins, provides possibilities for moral themes. *Fabliau* in Chaucer's case is a developed art.

A striking feature is his characterization. Many other *fabliaux* were simply anecdotes in which the events were mentioned but without developing the characters as possible real people. Having looked at the summaries of other *fabliaux* plots, in the Appendix pp. 166-7, do you sense that Chaucer succeeded in adding elements which made plot, realism and character, all more meaningful?

Settings and Other Uses of Realism

Although the story that The Miller tells is far-fetched, the various settings for the events are in many ways realistic. What is usually meant by the term 'realism' when we apply it to Chaucer? Charles Muscatine in his essay, 'Style of the Man and Style of the Work' (see Brewer, ed. 1966, p. 105), describes Chaucer's realism in this way:

> [the realism] asserts in various ways the primacy of matter and of animal nature in human concerns; accordingly, [it is a style] compounded of domestic imagery, natural discourse, local setting.

To us in the Twentieth century, when we try and define realism, we think of places, people and events which, good or bad, liked or disliked, we can genuinely see in our minds. In medieval life it was not so much visualizing people and places as real that mattered, but the importance of including traits of behaviour in literature, which would not normally have been there. Realism tended to create a more basic and earthy interpretation of human behaviour than did rhetoric, elevated description and other more lofty styles of writing. To put it at a more crude level, Chaucer was introducing his reader to the reality that human beings did not live just by fine emotions and moral purposes, but that they had bodily functions, they ate, excreted, had sex, they cooked, drank, laboured, lived in real places, and that life could be comic as well as noble. His poetry also recognizes that ordinary people lived amongst domestic objects, in the countryside as well as in towns, that they travelled about locally to do business and that the lives of ordinary people were encompassed by work, tasks and chores. This would surely have been all the more potent as Chaucer's readers were likely to have been mostly in court or professional circles – there was certainly not the mass readership which devours true-to-life stories nowadays.

Chaucer's realism is a remarkable display of his knowledge of the world outside the court. He spent a varied professional life: as well as his many associations with the royal household, he travelled a lot, fought in France and he also worked in customs. Perhaps it was this variety that enabled him to understand what really happened in medieval life.

One of the best examples of this detailed knowledge is the section of *The Miller's Tale* when Absolon goes to Gerveys' forge to borrow the iron blade. Quite apart from the way that Absolon's early morning errand is brought vividly to life: *A softe paas he wente over the strete* (652), there is a lifelike impression of the blacksmith at work. Gerveys' role is not untypical in Chaucer's poetry. He is quite independent of the action, and yet his contribution, without his realizing it, will play a prominent part. His work is described in close detail:

> That in his forge smythed plough harneys;
> He sharpeth shaar and kultour bisily.   (654–5)

This hints ironically at the sharp pain soon to be inflicted on Nicholas. Gerveys takes a frivolous view of Absolon's appearance so early in the morning at his forge. Again, we see the heightened realism in his speech:

> ... Som gay gerl, God it woot,
> Hath broght yow thus upon the viritoot.   (661–2)

This jocularity leads him to ask the ironically naive question: '*What wol ye do therwith?*' (674).

In other tales, Chaucer uses minor characters in similar roles: presenting an aspect of medieval society realistically, and adding irony through their brief involvement in events of the stories.

Elsewhere in the poem, we get the impression that Chaucer knew about the work of a carpenter, and quite a lot about astronomy. The world of work is an important feature of *The Miller's Tale*: there are many examples of characters going about their daily business, leading to an added awareness of the social class of individuals.

Activity

This activity is in two parts.
(a)   Realism is used in different ways in *The Miller's Tale*. The settings come to life, as do the actions of many of the characters.

Using the following examples, identify phrases which make the poem so lifelike: the description of Nicholas' room (100–05); the description of Alison's clothes (127–35); the moment when John's knave, Robyn, goes up to the attic (331–5), and then later when he returns to it (360–3); and the section describing the hanging of the kneading troughs (512–21). Can you find other sections which are especially realistic?

(b) Identify where the important action takes place: first, within or at John's house (remember that some of it takes place outside his bedroom casement), and second, elsewhere.

Discussion

These questions and pointers might help you to consider the realism of setting and actions. What are we told at the beginning of the story about the home of the carpenter? Does it add to the realism that he should take a lodger? Nicholas, we learn, had a *chambre...in that hostelrye* (95). Notice that because most of the important action takes place in John's house, or beneath the casement window there is a certain style of dramatic humour in the tale, rather in the way that the action of a modern dramatic farce often takes place in and out of domestic rooms, especially bedrooms.

As for actions, how do they reflect the everyday events in the lives of the characters? Notice that John goes away for a day to a real place, – to *Oseneye* (166). Absolon works as a *parissh clerk* (204) at the *paryssh chirche* (199) and that is where he sets eyes on Alison. What does Absolon's visit to the blacksmith contribute to the tale's sense of reality?

Another kind of realism in the description of action lies in the 'raciness' of some of the behaviour. When John has gone to Osney, back at his house Nicholas wastes no time grabbing hold of Alison. How does he grab hold of her, by which part of her body? Are we shocked by this? If so, why? What do you make of Chaucer's style when he is describing Absolon's visits to Alison's window?

Consider time locations. After the introductions, Nicholas and Alison's relationship starts at a particular time:

...so bifel the cas
That on a day this hende Nicholas   (163–4)

but they agree to wait for their adultery to take place. Nicholas begins his deception on a particular day, a Saturday, and stays in his room all weekend. Can you find other specific references to time? What contrasts exist between night and day, for example?

Another feature is the use of commonplace objects. In lines 332-3 we are given a clear visual impression of the door into Nicholas' room. What is it that supplies this impression? Characters refer to familiar, everyday objects. Sometimes this is contrasted, ironically, with other styles of speech. A good example of this is in John's long speech to Nicholas when he is outside his chamber (341–59). Look at the final lines of this speech. Most of what he says has been far-fetched, spoken with all the passion of an invocation. But in the final three lines, he reverts to an unconstrained request to get Robyn to break down the door:

'Get me a staf, that I may underspore,
Whil that thou, Robyn, hevest up the dore.'   (357-8)

The language and objects of everyday living are used in the planning for the flood. Once again realism mingles with irony. It is an absurd undertaking, but the planning is meticulous, just as if John the carpenter were going about a job of work for a valued customer:

He gooth and geteth hym a knedyng trogh,
And after that a tubbe and a kymelyn,   (512–3)

and:

His owene hand he made laddres thre,
To clymben by the ronges and the stalkes.   (516–7)

Can you see how on these occasions, realism is often set against implausibility? The contrasts of styles are striking. Think of Chaucer's styles (i.e. throughout *The Canterbury Tales*) as being versatile and flexible. The phrase 'mixed style' has been used to summarize his work, suggesting that he can readily move between elevated language when the occasion demands, and a more familiar everyday sort of realism when he needs to. As you study *The Miller's Tale* try to understand the way that courtly, rhetorical and romantic styles of writing are set alongside the detailed realism. The more you can grasp this contrast, the easier it should be to understand the element of parody in the tale.

Animalism

This is a term often used to describe some of the gross realism. The story is about sex. It is not the type of sex which is suggestive in a romantic or sensual way, but sexual behaviour which is unashamedly coarse and ribald. This comes as no surprise. The Miller himself has already been presented as a man of animal traits. Look back at the portrait of him in the extract from the *General Prologue* p. 1. The imagery used to describe his beard and the colour of the hair sticking out from the wart on his nose pictures him as a fox and a sow! We learn, hardly surprisingly, that the stories he told were mostly of *synne and harlotries* (*General Prologue* [561]). Perhaps the descriptions of his uncontrolled brawn, and indeed his drunkenness, add to our impression of him as a character who behaves as much like a beast as a man.

In the story itself, there is no mistaking the energy for sexual advances in some of the characters, even if the sex itself is rather glossed over in the language. The behaviour of Alison and Nicholas is frequently presented with a sudden burst of energy in the pace and style of the verse which becomes coarse and frank, and which, if it were not being spoken by The Miller, would be shocking.

Look at the passage beginning at line 163. What do you make of the fact that Nicholas *Fil with this yonge wyf to rage and pleye,* (165)? Notice that he catches her *by the queynte* (168) and her response, described in a direct animal simile, is to spring *as a colt dooth in the trave* (174). A few lines later, as they hatch their plan to beguile John, he pats her around the loins.

Immediately after this racy incident, The Miller introduces Absolon, quite a different kind of sexual being to Nicholas. But even here the poem remains animalistic. Towards the end of the description which introduces this rather pretentious character, The Miller wrily lets it be known that *he was somdeel squaymous / Of fartyng* (229–30). As you know from later on in the story, this problem is going to affect him in a most unlikely way. In fact, his phobia is introduced into the structure of the tale just as the teller of a dirty joke might have done: it is hardly something we would have expected; it contrasts pointedly with what we have learnt about his courtliness, and it is surely going to be referred to again – something for us to remember as the joke reaches its climax.

Animalism plays its part early in the story: then notice how vividly it surfaces later. Once Nicholas has the opportunity, he rushes Alison into bed with him: *Withouten wordes mo they goon to bedde* (542). They descend from the attic as soon as John has dropped off to sleep *Aboute corfew-tyme* (537). How long do you think there might have been between curfew time and the early morning service of 'laudes'?

Then, as Absolon waits for the first crowing of the cock, he recognizes his amorous feelings partly because his mouth has been itching all day, and all night he has dreamed of being at a feast. As he offers his plaintive love suit at her casement he reveals that he longs for Alison *as dooth a lamb after the tete* (596). As she comes to the window, his mouth becomes drier and drier and he ends up kissing *hir naked ers* (626)! At this point of the poem, The Miller holds back nothing in the extreme realism of his style. We are told the full details of what Absolon does as he is forced to bring his mouth into contact with Alison's pubic hair: *He felte a thyng al rough and long yherd,* (630).

The next scene at the window is even more coarse. Nicholas rises *for to pisse* (690); he wants to add to the fun by getting Absolon to *kisse his ers er that he scape* (692); there is then an extremely vivid description of his backside hanging out of the window; and all of this reaches a comic climax with the lines which recall, to the alert listener, Absolon's earlier mentioned phobia:

> This Nicholas anon leet fle a fart
> As greet as it had been a thonder-dent,   (698–9)

The physical nature of the tale continues as the *hoote kultour* (704) is brandished by Absolon to burn the skin off Nicholas' rump.

Just as the versatility of style is noted, it is often claimed of *The Canterbury Tales* as a whole that here was a poem capable of revealing all sides of human nature. Elsewhere in the tales, Chaucer reveals that human beings love money, that they are driven by pride, that they can be pompous and hypocritical, devious and scheming, noble and brave. His tales reveal an endless grasp of the motives behind so much of human behaviour. In *The Miller's Tale*, when realistic human behaviour becomes 'animalistic', might he be suggesting that human beings, especially when driven strongly by sexual desires, are capable of acting more like beasts?

Approaches through Character

Characterization

Characterization is important in *The Miller's Tale*. Each of the four main characters is presented in a highly individualized way. In *The Knight's Tale*, the lovers had a role to play as part of the romance, but they were not brought to life as real characters in the same vivid manner as the characters are in *The Miller's Tale*. In fact, the introductions to the characters by The Miller are reminiscent of the portraits of the pilgrims in the *General Prologue*, in which Chaucer uses a number of techniques to describe his characters. The characters are to some extent stock types, but also they become increasingly individualized as the events of the story unfold.

Each character is interesting individually, but they are all also connected with each other, and much of the humour, and the themes of the story, stem from these various connections. The jealous, ageing husband who is over-possessive of his younger wife is on the receiving end of an elaborate joke which makes a cuckold of him, whilst the squeamish clerk is also made to appear a complete fool by the two clever adulterers, and yet the tables are turned on them by his revengeful scheme. Like other tales, from all times, which tell of the hopes and woes of suitors who have fallen for the same woman, the story demands these characters to plot against each other or to be the victims of someone else's plot.

John

John, 'the carpenter', fills a role in the *fabliau* of the jealous husband. He is a good example of a stock, or stereotype, character who increasingly becomes individualized. He is rich, but stupid, and his gullibility provides the chance for the main practical joke of the story. He has foolishly married a wife much younger than himself, a mismatch likely to cause jealousy and resentment for any spouse in the same position, but catastrophic for one so naive and inept with his emotions, and so untrusting of his young wife. In the introduction to John, starting at line 113, his possessiveness and stupidity are hinted at, as well as the unfortunate contrast between *his* age and *her* youth:

> Jalous he was, and heeld hire narwe in cage,
> For she was wylde and yong, and he was old.   (116–17)

Through the image of his keeping her in a cage, we see how much he restrained and controlled her, because of his jealousy, although there is also irony in this restraint because it is precisely in her *cage* (116) – i.e. his house, where she is tempted to go behind his back. There are further indications of his stupidity. It is unlikely that he would have known the teachings of Cato, *That bad man sholde wedde his simylitude* (120), but nevertheless, by mention of this, his ignorance is drawn to our attention, and, more directly, we are also told that his *wit was rude* (119). At the end of this introductory section to John, an animal image is again used, this time about him directly:

> But sith that he was fallen in the snare,
> He moste endure, as oother folk, his care.   (123-4)

Who is actually trapped, John, or his wife?

John's ignorance contrasts with the wit and scholarship of Nicholas. Do you get an impression, in these lines of introduction, that John has little control over his life? If he has to *endure…his care* (124), what does that suggest about him? Is he the sort of character who lives at the mercy of other people manipulating and controlling him? Whilst this appears to be the case at home, where he is duped by his wife and by the scholarship of his lodger, we can derive a totally opposite impression from what we learn about him as a carpenter. He takes admirable control in responding to the threat of the flood, and we also learn that he is highly respected locally as a carpenter, both by implication that his unfortunately timed absence was due to a call on his trade at Osney, and through what we learn about him from the lines spoken by the cloisterer to Absolon, (556–62). (See Notes p.73.) His inadequacies would appear to affect him more in his personal than his working life. Does this affect the way we see Nicholas' success as a practical joker?

When Nicholas begins to fool John with his elaborate and carefully-worked plan, John is worried about his lodger, shut away in his room, and responds with a tone of anxiety which sharply reveals his limited and gullible nature. As well as worrying that Nicholas may die, he complains of the world as being unstable, almost as if he cannot get anything right: *'This world is now ful tikel, sikerly.'* (320). He appears to worry not only about Nicholas, but about the world in general, characteristic possibly of his age – a man full of woe, with little enjoyment in life. This rather woebegone nature is brought out in his own morbid example:

> 'I saugh today a cors yborn to chirche
> That now, on Monday last, I saugh hym wirche.'   (321-2)

(This terrible feeling of the instability of life was characteristic of medieval life. It is revealed in other writing of the period, and by Chaucer in other tales.)

John's foolishness is increasingly revealed as he is the subject of Nicholas' well-worked practical joke. The lofty, insistent style of Nicholas' rhetoric is too persuasive for John to resist. Whatever his skills as a carpenter, Chaucer never really allows the reader to sympathize with this poor man. Although in the end he comes to no real harm, he is mocked mercilessly and what he is forced into doing by Nicholas reveals the level of gullibility which we suspected in the opening description of him, although of course it allows him to use the many skills he possesses in his working life. It is important that he should not be accepted too sympathetically or the enjoyment of the ribald joke played by Nicholas and Alison would be diminished.

As well as being naive, John is also sincere. There is evidence of this in the blessings he offers Nicholas between lines 341 and 352. This passage, and the following lines, are full of irony. He rejects Nicholas' learnedness and extols the virtues of the simple man who has only his creed to guide him, without desiring to look further into the secrets of *Goddes pryvetee* (346). Ironically, whilst he speaks these very words, it is John himself whose simple beliefs are leading him into the trap of being made a *cokewold* (118).

(There is, however, another irony in this part of the tale. This is that Nicholas will later suffer, and perhaps in a more painful way than John.)

A contrast between the characterization of John and Nicholas comes about when John asks his knave, Robyn, to *hevest up the dore* (358). When the door has been knocked down, Nicholas sits *ay as stille as stoon* (364), confidently in control of his cunning plan, playing out the part with ingenuity and conviction. John, in all sincerity , and in tones of deep concern, tries to wake him from his trance. To save Nicholas from the wicked evil spirits which seem to have possessed him, in an absurd set of actions, he superstitiously offers charms to his house in order to drive away the evil spirits which he thinks have visited it, and calls upon the help of saints to bless it against the intrusion of wicked creatures. This incident has followed the point when John berates Nicholas for the folly of his studying: *'He shal be rated of his studyng.'* (355). Who in your opinion is the bigger fool at this point in the tale?

Activity

Nicholas persuades John of the coming flood and of the need to take ridiculous precautions against it. Explore John's reactions to the plan and show how his character is further revealed through his actions and speech as he falls for the joke.

Discussion

I find all the features of John's character concentrated in the section beginning at line 503. His absurd behaviour is explained once again by the jealous love he has for his wife, confirming what we learnt earlier, that he will behave irrationally as a result of his devotion to Alison. This insight is delivered in an elevated style (quite the opposite of realism) to suggest that human behaviour is controlled by powerful human emotions: *Lo, which a greet thyng is affeccioun!* (503).

Following what we learn about the way that John's emotions control him, we then discover the very practical side to his character. Having got over his *sory cheere* (510), he sets about the task of saving his family from the coming flood with enormous professional skill. Furthermore, he carefully provides food and drink for his confinement, and so is in a state of as much readiness for the coming disaster as he possibly could be. Chaucer confirms his practical disposition in the line: *[he]...dressed alle thyng as it sholde be.* (527). Is there a contradiction or contrast implied in this: as a character, is he foolish of mind yet so clever of hand? His simple, religious but superstitious faith is once again brought out as he says his prayers and awaits the onset of the rain; yet he should know there could be no second flood.

Finally, it occurs to me that there is a reminder of his age. Notice that he falls asleep at curfew time. Is another contrast implied by this, remembering what Nicholas and Alison are doing at the time?

Nicholas

Nicholas is one of the liveliest and cleverest characters in *The Canterbury Tales*. His introduction suggests a complex character, and certainly somebody quite capable of outwitting the simple-minded carpenter. As well as being a scholar he is also given an individualizing characteristic through his hobby of astrology. This is something he is going to use as a main part of the joke he plays on John. The study of astrology was popular in Chaucer's society, but his interest in the subject may have been included for other reasons. Consider carefully what we are told about his hobby:

> ...but al his fantasye
> Was turned for to lerne astrologye,
> And koude a certeyn of conclusiouns,
> To demen by interrogaciouns,
> If that men asked hym, in certein houres
> Whan that men sholde have droghte or elles shoures,
> Or if men asked hym what sholde bifalle
> Of every thyng; I may nat rekene hem alle.   (83-90)

The impression is of a character who thoroughly enjoys the calculations and speculations which are part of astrology. As we observe his clever manipulation of the unfortunate John during the tale, we may be forgiven for thinking that he enjoys the workings of his deception as much as its end result, the prize of a night with Alison. His enjoyment of the intrigue in his plan may be the reason why he does not go to bed with Alison when he first has his chance. There are two prizes that he wants: one is a night with Alison, what is the other?

103

Returning to his introduction, the complexity of his character is then built-up with some carefully-selected features, all of which play their part in his behaviour during the remainder of the tale. A sly, secretive man, he took great pleasure in adulterous behaviour, again suggesting that the scheming of adultery is just as important to him as the results. There are then three elements to Nicholas' character which are expressed using similar techniques to those used by Chaucer in the descriptions of the pilgrims in the *General Prologue*: description of physical appearance; mention of possessions; a catalogue of accomplishments, or skills. His room smells sweetly of herbs and he too shows that he is conscious of his own body by adorning it to make it:

> ...as sweete as is the roote
> Of lycorys or any cetewale. (98-9)

Compare this with Absolon's fastidious preparations (582–4).

The way that his books, and the equipment used for astronomy are so carefully laid out, plus what we learn about his accomplished singing and musical skills, make Nicholas seem very successful as a scholar. It is also the first instance of mock-courtliness in the poem. Although not a courtier himself, he possesses many of the skills associated with courtly life. Above all, he is a character of immense self-confidence and ability. Perhaps most importantly though, he knows that he has these abilities. We sense a boldness and even arrogance about him, so that it may not altogether surprise us when he grabs hold of Alison in the crude way that he does, a little later in the poem.

Before considering the contribution that Nicholas makes to the story, I want to draw your attention to one word which has often been commented on as important in the understanding of Nicholas. That is the word *hende*. It is an adjective used many times to describe him, so much so that it is probably ironic. In essence it meant 'courteous', but with Nicholas it is usually assumed that his courtesy – considerable as it was – existed because he was so keen to win his way through to successful adulterous affairs. Thus, the word is so frequently repeated as a reminder that his grace and charm was calculated to seduce women and generally take people in. There does appear to be something in this idea. *Hende*, he possibly is, but there is another side to Nicholas' character which is far from charming or courtly. He is also crude and uncouth. His audacious sexual advance towards Alison and the way that he *leet fle a fart* (698) on the hapless Absolon, certainly both reveal another side to his character. *Hende* could also mean 'near at hand', which may suggest further irony to you, when you compare Nicholas' closeness to Alison, with John and Absolon's distance from the woman they love.

Activity

Following the introduction to Nicholas, it is his actions, and most especially, his speech, which characterize him. What do we learn about him from his actions and from the considerable amount of speech that he is given in the tale?

Pay particular attention to lines 393–502. What does Nicholas say to John, how does he say it, and with what effect?

Discussion

With John out of the way, Nicholas goes quickly into action, unceremoniously grabbing hold of Alison *by the queynte* (168), telling her that he will die for her love. Slightly rebuffed, he then becomes extremely charming: *And spak so faire, and profred him so faste*, (181), with the result that she gives in. We see his lust, his self-confident boldness and his courtly charm coming out in this passage, which is written in a style full of pace and energy. But what follows may be even more revealing of his character. Alison may have welcomed his advances, but she points out that, because John is such a jealous husband, he, Nicholas, is going to have to be secretive in the adultery. Is it at this point that Nicholas is revealed in his truest light?

> 'Nay, thereof care thee noght,' quod Nicholas.
> 'A clerk hadde litherly biset his whyle,
> But if he koude a carpenter bigyle.'   (190–2)

Nicholas is going to enjoy rising to the challenge of a plan set to beguile John. Is the delight in setting the trap going to be as rewarding as the pleasure he will gain from the adultery with Alison? Many critics have observed that, because John is away at Osney, there was nothing to stop them from their fornication at this point of the poem. Remember also that he had got hold of her crutch, and so his intentions were fairly clear. Why do they delay, especially when the plan to keep John at bay is such a complex one, and when you consider that it is going to put Nicholas to some trouble to set it in motion? In line 297, we read that the plot against John is a 'game'.

A feature of the plot is its sheer ingenuity. Nicholas' disappearance is enough to give the simple carpenter a sense that something is wrong, so he sends his servant, Robyn, up to Nicholas' room. He manages to look into the room through a hole in the wall. Consider the parody of Nicholas' behaviour at this point. For all the world he appears to be in a complete trance:

This Nicholas sat evere capyng upright,
As he had kiked on the newe moone. (336–7)

The deceit is later continued in an even more earnest and sophisticated way when Nicholas finally gets round to saying something to John. Somehow, by this point the entire prank will have seemed even more convincing to John, especially as he has had to get Robyn to break the door down to enter Nicholas' chamber. Nicholas has so carefully planned his plot that everything seems as normal as it possibly could be to the unsuspecting John.

In his speech to John, Nicholas combines tones of great frendliness with religious and scientific authority, plus a kind of moral blackmail, convincing the carpenter that Alison is in danger. He brings the horror of the flood to the front of his mind in a vivid and frightening picture and then convinces John, through some very practical discussion, of what he has to do to save himself and his wife from the disaster.

What Nicholas actually says to John is a wonderful example of rhetorical deception. It contains such a variety of persuasive techniques, so that the poor gullible John, foolish and simple man that he is, does not stand a chance. Nicholas' argument, based on the apparent authority of his astrological predictions plays on John's faith and fears:

'That now a Monday next, at quarter nyght,
Shal falle a reyn, and that so wilde and wood
That half so greet was nevere Noes flood.' (408–10)

Alison

In the manner of a courtly heroine, Alison is also introduced (lines 125–62) at length. She is beautiful and desirable, but unlike the real courtly heroines in the literature of her time, Alison is a country wench. Her attributes as a woman are described by using imagery from the countryside and farmyard, and what stands out in her introduction is the amount of animal imagery.

Her body is as slender and delicate *As any wezele* (126); her clothing suggests the decorative, starched prettiness of a country maiden; her headband is worn high, showing off her forehead; her physical appearance is twice compared to fruit trees; a beautifully adorned purse hangs down by her belt. Chaucer's descriptive language makes this busy country wench positively seductive and enticing:

> There nys no man so wys that koude thenche
> So gay a popelote or swich a wenche.   (145–6)

Activity

Look carefully at lines 149–62. In these lines there are many references to animals or nature. Identify these references. What sort of impression do they give you of Alison's character? Where else in the poem does Alison reveal natural or animalistic behaviour?

Discussion

Alison is a lively, flirtatious character; there is evidence of this in line 136: *And sikerly she hadde a likerous ye.*

Think about the lines which come at the end of the introduction to Alison:

> She was a prymerole, a piggesnye,
> For any lord to leggen in his bedde,
> Or yet for any good yeman to wedde.   (160–2)

What are we to conclude from these lines? That she is unlikely to marry a lord, likely to marry a yeoman, but likely to sleep with a lord?

The energy, and overtones of animalism in the latter part of the description of Alison are continued in the first main part of the action that she is involved in. When, a line or two later, Nicholas takes hold of her and starts to make arrangements for the seduction, her reaction is described in two of the finest descriptive lines of the poem, just as if she were a frisky young horse:

> And she sproong as a colt dooth in the trave,
> And with her heed she wryed faste awey,　　　　　　(174–5)

There is also further evidence in this part of the tale of mock courtliness. She rejects Nicholas' advances in language that is quite exaggerated and melodramatic, playing out a kind of ritual with him reminiscent of behaviour typical of courtly lovers:

> ...'I wol nat kisse thee, by my fey!
> Why, lat be!' quod she. 'Lat be, Nicholas,
> Or I wol crie "out, harrow" and "allas"!　　　　　　(176–8)

Does it surprise you that, in spite of this melodramatic rejection, she should be ready to accept him almost immediately?

A few further ideas about Alison: does the description of her appearance in lines 202–3 indicate why Absolon may have fallen for her? What do lines 541–8 tell us about her as an adulterous lover? Finally, did the nature and animal imagery prepare us for her most important contribution to the *fabliau* plot when *at the wyndow out she putte hir hole*, (624)? She finds it hilarious that Absolon should have *kiste hir naked ers* (626). She certainly shows no hesitation or shame at behaving in such a compromising way, and we suspect that if Nicholas had not stuck his own bum out of the window on the second occasion, she would have done the same again. Do you think that she may even have been trying to upstage Nicholas as a practical joker?

Absolon

The characterization of Absolon is closest to courtly parody. Nicholas has many varied attributes; indeed he is a complex character, and in the way that he reacts to his initial rejection by Alison, he imitates the classic behaviour of the rejected courtly lover. Alison pays the kind of attention to herself which is associated with the courtly heroine, but neither of them quite aspires to courtliness in their basic habits in the same extreme way as does Absolon.

He is intensely self-conscious, to the point of affectation, and very aware of his appearance. To understand this, consider the attention he pays to his hairstyle:

> Crul was his heer, and as the gold it shoon,
> And strouted as a fanne large and brode;
> Ful streight and evene lay his joly shode.   (206–8)

It has been suggested that he is described as effeminate. There are hints of this in the animal imagery used to describe his appearance: in addition to his hair which resembled a peacock's fan, notice that his eyes were *greye as goos* (209). These seem rather different kinds of animal images to those used to describe the liveliness of Alison. Their whole tone is much more refined and reserved, in keeping with the shyness which consumed this man's character.

Absolon's proud and fanciful approach to life is confirmed in the classic Chaucerian description of his clothing. The descriptions of his shoes, hose, tunic and gown are full of delicate colours and nature imagery, giving an overall impression of a very fastidious man.

If he *looked* the part of a courtly lover then he could also *behave* like one. He could dance, he could play musical instruments, he could sing – even if this was with a rather high-pitched voice, perhaps another hint of his effeminacy! Whilst we remain suspicious as to how far he was successful, he was a womanizer of sorts, or at least saw himself as one. But even though he entertained all the barmaids of the town with his accomplished singing, he was saving himself for Alison, the carpenter's wife. He is described as having a *love-longynge* (241) for Alison. Like a truly practised and intent courtier, unable to sleep at night, he would go to her window and sing *in his voys gentil and smal* (252):

> 'Now, deere lady, if thy wille be,
> I praye yow that ye wole rewe on me.'   (253–4)

What might Absolon's biblical namesake tell us about his character? Refer to Notes on p. 50.

Activity

Look closely at the description of Absolon's efforts to woo Alison in lines 263–76. What sort of lover is Absolon? How well does he play the part of a romantic courtly hero?

Discussion

Absolon fits into a tradition of characters in literature which is about courtly love. This was sometimes called *fine amour*. An activity which often involved the pursuit of somebody else's wife, it was a series of attentions which treated women with the highest of respect. It was amorous behaviour which involved a sort of craft, or code, full of ritual and message designed to attract the woman, often involving cultural and artistic accomplishments such as poetry, song and dance. The very act of offering love in this manner would be a way of ennobling the courtier, and yet the woman would be expected to reject him and make herself an ever greater prize for the lover's advances. Sometimes this ritual of love games could lead to outcomes of tragic intensity, on other occasions it was simply farce.

In the passage that describes Absolon's attempts to woo Alison, consider the attention he pays to her, the gifts he offers her and the dramatic tone of what he has to say to her. Do you think he is capable of being seductive?

Chaucer belittles Absolon's attempts to play the courtly lover with a reminder that all this amorous activity is really rather pointless:

> But what availleth hym as in this cas?
> She loveth so this hende Nicholas
> That Absolon may blowe the bukkes horn;
> He ne hadde for his labour but a scorn. (277–80)

This rejection may add to the parody of Absolon's behaviour: the more earnest he is in his games of courtly love behaviour, the more he is making a fool of himself because the woman loves another (and not her husband)!

As Absolon's role develops through the rest of the tale, we see him deceiving himself that he is in with a chance with Alison. This seems quite significant to me. He has not seen John stir after the foolish carpenter has shut himself away in his attic, and he interprets this as an opportunity:

> This Absolon ful joly was and light,
> And thoghte, 'Now is tyme to wake al nyght,
> For sikirly I saugh hym nat stirynge
> Aboute his dore, syn day bigan to sprynge.' (563–6)

When on this occasion he goes to Alison's window, the techniques of characterization are marked. From lines 579–99, Chaucer hints strongly at the physical characteristics in Absolon's preparations as a lover. The way that he has sweetened his breath, and the way that he complains to her as he grows faint, sweating and longing for her *as dooth a lamb after the tete* (596), all contribute to a picture of Absolon as a man very conscious of his own appearance and with a strong physical presence as a lover (at least that is his self-image).

How this contrasts with his physical reactions to the disappointment he is about to experience! The true Absolon who springs back in disgust from his unfortunate kiss is suddenly a very different kind of character to the accomplished courtier we have supposedly seen throughout the poem so far. We might have been prepared for this pathetic reversal when we learnt earlier of his squeamishness, and there is an even more subtle way in which his prowess as a courtly lover is mocked. On the evening before he first goes to Alison's window, he decides to take a nap, but in fact oversleeps, hardly the sign of a true and ardent lover. There is a juxtaposition of the lines:

'Therfore I wol go slepe an houre or tweye,
And al the nyght thanne wol I wake and pleye.'   (577–8)
with:
Whan that the firste cok hath crowe, anon
Up rist this joly lovere Absolon,   (579–80)

Are we also prepared for his revenge? His quest to get hold of the *hoote kultour* (668) and the way he uses it leads him to take the skin off another man's buttocks, an action we learn from the incident at Gerveys' forge, that he fully intended, with no scruples whatsoever for the pain or outcome. What do you make of this vicious behaviour? Is it to be interpreted merely as a part of the comic plot, or does it express other features of Absolon's character?

One of the roles of Gerveys the blacksmith – to contribute to the realism of the tale – is discussed in the Approaches p.94, but another reason for sketching his manner of behaviour as so easy-going and unvexed, may be to provide a contrast with the now terse and single-minded Absolon. Indeed, are we to interpret Absolon's vicious intentions as more purposeful than his earlier amorous activities? In the end, he has certainly gained revenge, but does that make us sympathetic towards him as a character? I suspect not.

The Action

The action of the tale cannot be separated from the characters. Neither can we consider the characters, their actions, or the plot, without an understanding of parody. You may find it helpful to read the section on parody (Approaches pp. 126–8 and also the Notes pp. 44–5, and p. 50), which will help you to realize that throughout the poem, Chaucer is imitating a courtly romance in a humorous way.

The structure of the plot is a mixture of the plausible and the outrageous. A lot of it is clearly imaginable, (see the section on Realism, p. 93). The rest is plain farce. The structure also depends on the development of each character's desire or obsession: John's to save himself, but more especially Alison, from the coming flood; Absolon's to woo Alison; Alison's to bed Nicholas; Nicholas to succeed in his plan to fool John and, of course, to sleep with Alison. Each part of the plot is separately developed and then brought together in the climactic moment at the end when Nicholas is branded and John hoaxed. It may be helpful to refer back to the Discussion section on settings and time locations, pp. 95–6, to be reminded of how the structure of events allows for brief forays out into the community – all of which depict realistic medieval life, although most of the more farcical action takes place in John's house. Notice too how the plot is full of surprises. This is partly due to the mixture of styles which make up the tale, and in particular the juxtaposition of realism and farce. The result is that we can be reading a sequence of the tale which seems plausible and then all of a sudden, something outrageous or farcical happens. The result is a striking mixture of authentic representation of medieval life with incredible comedy.

Nicholas' sudden and bold attempt to seduce Alison comes into this category of surprising behaviour, and then later in the poem, the swift transition from mock courtly romance to crude farce, as Absolon kisses Alison's rear, quickly moves the poem into a new and unexpected vein. Whilst we might have been smiling wrily at Absolon's foolish courtliness, we are all of a sudden guffawing raucously at the sheer bawdiness of the action.

I have suggested that we cannot separate the action from the characters. It is also noticeable that the action depends such a lot on the ways that the behaviour of one character affects another. Any action is either an attempt to deceive another character, or a reaction to the deceptions of others. Really only the three minor characters act in a way that can be interpreted as entirely independent of other characters, although even Gerveys is unwittingly engaged in a contribution to the farce and the cloisterer who speaks to Absolon similarly encourages him to go ahead with his fateful plan as a suitor. These sorts of connections between the characters are a feature of good comedy and farce, which depends on secrecy, practical jokes and deceptions.

Activity

Make a list of the instances of 'beguiling' that take place. Be sure to state exactly who is making a fool of whom, and what they are doing to make fools of others. Clearly, Nicholas and Absolon are going to be prominent as the 'beguilers', but what about Alison – will you include her?

Discussion

Think about the fact that a lot of the action involving one of the characters has the effect of reminding us of the plight or plans of another. John's jealous possession of his wife makes the plan hatched by Nicholas all the more striking. The fiasco of Absolon's love-suit is nothing to do with Alison's devotion to her husband, but is a flop from the start because of her adulterous devotion to Nicholas, and in this sense Absolon and Nicholas are finally connected, without actually having anything to do with each other.

It might also have occurred to you that all, or nearly all the action, is determined by the fact that this is, above all, a sexual comedy, and the motives for virtually all the behaviour of the characters originate in their sexual desires and feelings. Consider the evidence in the language used to express these dominant sexual forces. There is the jealousy of John:

Jalous he was, and heeld hire narwe in cage,   (116)

113

the erotic appetite of Nicholas:

> ...on a day this hende Nicholas
> Fil with this yonge wyf to rage and pleye,   (164–5)

the physical vibrancy of Alison:

> And she sproong as a colt dooth in the trave,   (174)

and the love-longing of Absolon:

> This parissh clerk, this joly Absolon,
> Hath in his herte swich a love-longynge   (240–1)

('Love longing' was a kind of lover's disease commonly expressed in courtly behaviour in the Fourteenth century – no self-respecting courtier chasing women would have failed to suffer from the disease!)

The action connects three men with one woman in a parody of courtly love. The ultimate aim of the men's labours is sex (or in John's case, preventing others from having sex with his wife).

Approaches through Themes and Topics

Destiny and Justice

Perhaps with the exception of Alison, none of the main characters concludes the tale in a situation they would have wished upon themselves at the start, although because this is comedy, the recriminations are not too severe at the end. Alison is the exception because she has enjoyed her night of passion with Nicholas, has rebuffed the irritating courtship of Absolon, and her marriage, as far as we are led to believe, remains intact. But even she could not have anticipated how events would have panned out, and it was perhaps chance which took Nicholas' buttocks to the casement rather than hers on the second occasion of Absolon's visit, saving her from the indignation and pain that he had in mind. It could even be argued that Alison is contemptuously denied a punishment, as if to emphasize her sinfulness.

But what of the others? Has John been foolish to marry a wife much younger than himself, and, given his jealous nature, is it just that he should be made such a fool? Does Nicholas' arrogance and cleverness – remember that he was a clerk of some considerable intelligence – merit being ridiculed in such a painful and humiliating way? And should Absolon's squeamish foppery lead to his being such a failure as a courtier and lover? In thinking about these questions, it may occur to you that the punishments for each character – if punishments they are – are extreme. Are they appropriate?

Human destiny, by its nature a very wide and grand theme, is important in many of *The Canterbury Tales*. Chaucer was interested in looking at the ways that the motivations and dispositions of individuals could affect the world, and how fate and chance events could play a part in determining the lives and futures of his characters.

As for the structure and tone of *The Miller's Tale*, there is evidence early on that destiny will be a key theme. In the descriptions of the main characters, there are a number of tensions and contradictions which set up a kind of argument which the plot will need to resolve. The most prominent of these tensions is clearly the mismatch in the marriage:

For she was wylde and yong, and he was old   (117)

As if to reinforce this discord, we soon learn, in an image that suggests Alison's irrepressible sexuality:

Fair was this yonge wyf, and therwithal
As any wezele hir body gent and smal.   (125–6)

As a result of the full and complex description of Nicholas' bumptious character it is difficult not to think that he needs to be cut down to size – to be taken down a peg or two! Chaucer carefully places the description of the *hende* Nicholas alongside the animalistic and rather lusty portrait of Alison, when we already know that her husband is a stupid man, worried anyway that he will be made a *cokewold* (118).It is small wonder that Nicholas and Alison will be connected with each other in the main part of the plot.

There is no natural connection between Absolon and Nicholas. Indeed, Absolon is introduced into the story as an extra character, and he knows nothing about Nicholas' role. It is hard to imagine in any work of literature two characters who become more intimately connected with each other, without once meeting, although clearly Alison tells Nicholas who Absolon is.

Chaucer leaps from the events at John's house in the early part of the story, to an introduction of Absolon, through the device of telling us that Alison went to the parish church on a holy day. This provides the opportunity to introduce Absolon:

> Now was ther of that chirche a parissh clerk,
> The which that was ycleped Absolon. (204-5)

Absolon's *love-longynge* (241) takes him to the hinged-window on John's wall, there to plead with Alison to take mercy on his desires for her. In mock-courtly fashion, he is seeking adulterous love, but all the while his assumption is that this will be at the expense of Alison's husband, John, and he knows nothing about the real love plot that is going on in secret. Ironically, John is stirred to express minor irritation at Absolon's activities:

> 'What! Alison! Herestow nat Absolon,
> That chaunteth thus under oure boures wal?' (258–9)

He will remain foolishly unaware of the real sexual plot about to take place, as will Absolon of the real rivalry that stands in the way of his success.

What we have is a series of incidents involving the characters which take place in ignorance of what others are up to. They are all destined towards a dramatic (and in Nicholas' case, a painful) climax as a result of their characteristics and behaviour. The creator of these destinies is the story-teller (Chaucer through his Miller). He hints throughout at the illusions suffered by the characters, and their shortcomings, which will lead them to their destinies. Nicholas has no contingency plan, and however good he is at using astrology to predict, or pretend to predict, the future for others, he fails to predict his own; John thinks that his wife is 'caged'; and Absolon holds a ridiculous perception of himself as a successful suitor. And all the while, their strongest character traits are too strong to allow them to see where they are going wrong.

Activity

Consider the climax of events (line 678 onwards) and deal with each of the following points:

(a)   is Absolon's treatment too severe a punishment?

(b)   even allowing for the element of farce, is Nicholas' violent destiny just reward for his clever trickery and adultery?

(c)   They seyde,'The man is wood, my leeve brother';
      And every wight gan laughen at this stryf.   (740–1)
      John has been completely deceived. Is this fair?

(d)   is Alison let off lightly?

Discussion

The themes in the tale cannot really be taken too seriously. One of the important features of the comic form that Chaucer uses for the story is a sense of resolution in spite of some fairly unusual happenings. Hence, the conclusion involves a rather light-hearted summary when, in another kind of tale, the various deceptions and tricks could have produced a more venomous ending:

Thus swyved was this carpenteris wyf,
For al his kepyng and his jalousye,
And Absolon hath kist hir nether ye,
And Nicholas is scalded in the towte.
This tale is doon, and God save al the rowte!   (742–6)

One feature of the tale is farce, and our enjoyment of the story is simply through laughter. But there is another side to it, and this is the way that the characters exhibit weaknesses and shortcomings in their personalities which deserve mocking. The question you have to ask yourself is: how successful has Chaucer been at identifying and revealing their faults? But you will also need to be clear on this: if they are being judged, then what for?

John's deserts are simple. However we may look upon him, he appears stupid. His foolish marriage has led him to become jealous of his younger wife, and although he is conscious of the fact that he could be beguiled, he does nothing to prevent it happening. Indeed his concern for Nicholas exacerbates the problem for himself. He reveals that he is so obsessed with Alison, through his silly response to the idea of a flood:

This carpenter answerde, 'Allas, my wyf!
And shal she drenche? Allas, myn Alisoun!'
For sorwe of this he fil almoost adoun,
And seyde, 'Is ther no remedie in this cas?'   (414–17)

The elaborate design of Nicholas' plan completely deceives John: the more absurd it becomes, the more he believes it, and so at the end of it he moans pitifully about the possible impending disaster. The Miller sums up his stupidity with the words:

Men may dyen of ymaginacioun,
So depe may impressioun be take.   (504–5)

This follows John's earlier superstitions. He is a man of simple faith, utterly ripe for Nicholas' practical joke, and he ends up imagining the horror of *Noes flood* (410), when all along he is being completely beguiled.

As for Nicholas, perhaps the issue of justice connects not so much with what he does, but how he does it. He is so obviously cleverer than John, and he is attractive to Alison. But, as has been suggested before, he could so easily have had his way with her quite early in the poem, when John was first absent on a Saturday, in Osney. I do not think we want to judge him for his seduction. But what we might be concerned about is the extremity of his elaborate plan. When he says:

'A clerk hadde litherly biset his whyle,
But if he koude a carpenter bigyle.'   (191–2),

we realize that the poem is going to be sustained not through any interest in whether or not he will be able to sleep with Alison, but in the enjoyment of his bizarre plan. His plans for the dupe, his simulation of madness, his careful rhetorical language to John, plus the moral pressure he exerts knowing that John will look to his wife, all combine to become a cruel elaborate joke. In the end, it may be that we do accept his punishment. It is unlikely in the nature of such a story that he would not have suffered some sort of retribution. He is that breed of character who is unscrupulously clever. His punishment is entirely physical, and very painful at that.

If there is justice for Absolon, it may not be for his foolishness; there are some hints at deeper shortcomings in his personality other than his silly attempts at courtly behaviour, which are probably also being mocked. Are there doubts about Absolon's sexual ability? How might these lead you to the judgement that he is prone to self- deception? The clues come in all the physical references to Absolon. Notice in particular his hair, his complexion, the pitch of his voice, his striking phobia, the way he sweetens his breath. For me, the most revealing indication is suggested by the dryness of his lips as he approaches his kiss with Alison, suggesting a complete sexual nervousness which has been carefully covered up by his courtly rhetoric and gracious behaviour at her window.

The 'misplaced kiss', as it is sometimes rather politely referred to, is described entirely from Absolon's point of view, and is handled in a deliberately mocking, simplistic tone to infer his naivety. Forced to kiss *hir naked ers* (626), he backs away:

> ... and thoughte it was amys,
> For wel he wiste a womman hath no berd.
> He felte a thyng al rough and long yherd,
> And seyde, 'Fy! allas! what have I do?' (628–31)

What sort of impression does this give of his sexual prowess? What does he do to his lips following this 'kiss'? Is his squeamishness reinforced by his attempts to wipe away the effects of the unfortunate kiss? How does this reaction compare with the *love-longynge* (241) that he felt the night before? It is interesting that there is earlier an ironic pair of lines which can be contrasted with his wiping away the kiss from his lips:

> 'My mouth hath icched al this longe day;
> That is a signe of kissyng atte leeste.' (574–5)

No judgement of Alison is passed. What view are we therefore to hold of her? She is surely to blame partly, if not equally, with Nicholas for the adultery plot and the treatment of Absolon. Is the absence of judgement a form of silent contempt for her disloyalty? Or are we to accept as reasonable all that she has done, to understand that her desires are natural, especially as John is so much older than she is?

When we come to consider who makes the judgements, it is worth reconsidering the importance of *The Miller's Prologue* and then studying *The Reeve's Prologue*. The only indication we have of the pilgrims' reactions to *The Miller's Tale* comes from *The Reeve's Prologue*. (See Notes pp. 84–5.) The Reeve has a particular reason for being upset – to him the story has slurred the trade of carpenters. Mostly, from what he says, we learn that the majority of the pilgrims have accepted the story light-heartedly. Equally, it is difficult to believe that Chaucer intends us to give much credit to The Miller as a moral judge. It is more likely that he is to be held responsible for the bawdiness and humour. Remember that Chaucer has already had to apologize for having to relate his story. In *The Miller's Prologue*, Chaucer was unequivocal about his pilgrim: *The Millere is a cherl; ye knowe wel this.* (74).

Might Chaucer be the judge? Not necessarily. The story has been light-hearted, the resolution none too tragic or serious, even allowing for John's humiliation and the skin torn off Nicholas' bottom. Beneath the surface of this rude farce is Chaucer's awareness of the shortcomings of his characters. None of them was faultless: John too foolishly and proudly jealous; Nicholas over-ambitious; Absolon a deception to himself; Alison, flirtatious and unfaithful. Yet the tone, mainly of laughter, at the end of the tale, plus the description in *The Reeve's Prologue* of its acceptance, perhaps leaves the pilgrims as listeners, or us as readers, a choice. If we wish, we can laugh it off; if we prefer, we can take a moral view. You will also want to consider, in a following section, whether there is religious judgement involved in their punishments (see Approaches pp. 123–5).

Proverbs

One stylistic feature linked to a sense of destiny is The Miller's use of proverbs. Once or twice he takes the opportunity to philosophize about life's affairs, either with a proverb or with an image which is like a proverbial saying. The tone of these sayings fits well into the realistic style of narrative, almost as if The Miller were chatting directly to his audience. Given that there are other features of the story which suggest the theme of destiny – the parody of the world's destruction through the coming of the flood, the background of astrology, frequent references to saints and philosophers, thinkers and writers (St Thomas à Becket, St Paul, Cato, Aesop, Ptolemy) – it is possible to interpret these proverbial sayings as part of the underlying theme of destiny, raising questions and ideas about the fates of the characters, and stressing the role that knowledge and learning play in the conduct of everyday affairs. Do you find that there is perhaps a contrast between the allusions to wise words of fate and destiny on the one hand, and the stupidity of human behaviour in the tale?

Here are two examples of the proverbial language, the first of an actual proverb, the second a popular saying:

Men seyn right thus: 'Alwey the nye slye
Maketh the ferre leeve to be looth.'   (284–5)

He hadde moore tow on his distaf.   (666)

(See also the section on Imagery, Approaches p. 133.)

Activity

What do you think these proverbs and sayings mean? Make your own collection of proverbs and sayings from *The Miller's Tale*. What do you think each of these means?

Concealment

Much of the tale deals with actions and attitudes attributed to characters, that are kept secret from others. This theme of secrecy, or privacy, first surfaces right at the start of the tale in the account of Nicholas' interest in the art of astrology. He could determine the futures and fates of other people through the clever use of his scientific calculations. This lends him a mystique, a sort of incontestable expertize which he uses to such effect in the hoaxing of John later in the poem. As well as hearing about his mysterious hobby, we also know that *he was sleigh and ful privee* (93). He enjoys secrecy and stealth in his elaborate plan to fool John.

John, on the other hand, is partly sceptical of Nicholas' apparent depth of obscure knowledge. He lacks the sense to question the reliability of Nicholas' astrological prediction, and, if anything, his scepticism reinforces his faith in Nicholas. What he believes instead is that men should not delve too deeply into the truth of things:

Men sholde nat knowe of Goddes pryvetee.
Ye, blessed be alwey a lewed man
That noght but oonly his bileve kan!   (346–8)

This suggests a contrast between the complex secrecy involved in Nicholas' planning and the way that John by nature conceals nothing. Indeed, part of his gullibility arises from his tendency to be so open about everything. He admits that he is likely to be made a cuckold due to the problems of the age gap in his marriage. He shows genuine concern for Nicholas' state of health. He complies at great

121

length with all the suggestions to save himself and his wife from the impending flood. One of the main reasons for the success of the hoax is that Nicholas speaks to John in such an alluring way. Interestingly, Nicholas uses the word *pryvetee* (385) as he entices John to listen to his warnings. This takes John into his confidence:

> This Nicholas answerde, 'Fecche me drynke,
> And after wol I speke in pryvetee
> Of certeyn thyng that toucheth me and thee.'　　　　　(384–6)

The way that he convinces John is then entirely through the authority of his astrology, as if to stress a private world of knowledge that will convince the simple carpenter. John, remember, does not know any better than to believe Nicholas' ingenious calculations, and he finds the predictions all the more convincing for the confidentiality and apparent trusting tone of Nicholas' words:

> 'Now John,' quod Nicholas, 'I wol nat lye;
> I have yfounde in myn astrologye,
> As I have looked in the moone bright,
> That now...'　　　　　(405–8)

What happens between the two characters is that concealment is added to concealment. Nicholas convinces John of the flood; John accepts the need to keep quiet about it, and will not even tell Robyn or his maid, Gill; in the end it is John who behaves with the greater conviction that the whole affair needs to be handled secretively:

> And on the Monday, whan it drow to nyght,
> He shette his dore withoute candel-lyght,
> And dressed alle thyng as it sholde be.　　　　　(525–7)

Absolon's attempts at secret seduction allow the theme to become intertwined amongst all four of the main characters. Absolon's plan is to go to John's house *at cokkes crowe* (567), and *Ful pryvely knokken at his wyndowe* (568). His attempts at concealment are different to those used by Nicholas. Both are clerks involved in a secret seduction, but what comes across in the account of Absolon's efforts is the stupidity of his behaviour. A point of irony in the structure of the story is that he has no need to deceive John: John has already been deceived! He is trying to imitate the actions of a secret lover in the court, and to this end he prepares himself for a secret kiss, which would have been quite a conquest for him.

Activity

Does Absolon conceal the truth about his weaknesses from himself? If he is deceiving himself, does this help to explain his elaborate attempts to behave like a courtly lover?

Discussion

There are some quite important points to think about concerning Absolon's attempts at deception. There is evidence, already cited, to suggest that he was neither physically nor sexually as confident as he may, himself, have thought. In an elaborately-wrought part of the plot, he disturbs the adultery of Nicholas and Alison, but the truth of this is concealed from him. In a similar way to John, he is wrong about everything: he is not going to be a successful lover; Alison is already committing adultery; all his physical longings will be rewarded, not by requital of love, but by anal flatulence.

This is followed by Absolon's attempt at revenge. In the short scene with Gerveys, Absolon behaves in an exaggeratedly secretive manner:

'...What wol ye do therwith?'
'Thereof,' quod Absolon, 'be as be may.
I shal wel telle it thee to-morwe day.'   (674–6)

The real Absolon, as it were, is perhaps revealed through this bitter act of revenge, and this makes me think that he has lacked self-understanding earlier. What he does with the iron blade is the only thing he ever actually *does* at all in the poem. Earlier, all he has done is planned or dreamed. His secret dealings with Gerveys, and his approach to Alison when he returns to her window, present a sense of indignation and an attempt to restore his pride. In the end, he comes across as a man full of complex secrets, contradicting his apparent earlier confidence when he plays the part of the courtly lover.

Religion and Spiritual Moments

Much of the tale involves a religious parody. This, added to the courtly parody, helps to mock the actions of the characters, adding to

123

the sense of farce. The subject of astronomy, introduced early in the tale, points us in the direction of the story's spiritual themes. The knowledge of Nicholas' remarkable control over the world through his study of astrology sets the tone for an ironic story about inexplicable events. This itself is ironic, of course, as everything that happens is always explicable, even if absurd. Nicholas' skills are supposedly mystical:

> Or if men asked hym what sholde bifalle
> Of every thyng; I may nat rekene hem alle.   (89–90)

It may well be the truth that there is nothing to be grasped in Nicholas' astrology, and that it is all a hoax.

You have already seen how John reacts to Nicholas' apparent fit: his superstitious behaviour is farcically exaggerated, reinforcing the absurdity of the situation – remember that it is himself, John, who needs the blessings and help, and not the scheming Nicholas. In addition to this background of superstition, there is frequently an awareness of religious activity and values, although there is some controversy amongst Chaucerian critics as to whether we can judge the sins of the characters against the tale's overtly Christian background.

Nicholas' singing of *Angelus ad virginem* (108) suggests that he ought to be mindful of the immense love of God for man – most of what he does sins against it; Alison attends the *paryssh chirche,/ Cristes owene werkes for to wirche*, (199–200) an activity hardly in keeping with her more common mode of behaviour in the story; Nicholas' choice of subject for his hoax, i.e. the coming of a second flood, parodies a popular theme for medieval Mystery Plays, which were meant righteously to instruct the people; Absolon played the part of Herod in one of these Mystery Plays, and he wears a decoration of the window of St Paul's Cathedral on one of his shoes; the lovers are still engaged in the sin of adultery at the point when, at line 548, local people were being called to prayer by the ringing of the bell for laudes.

These religious allusions give rise to the idea that the tale has a strong Christian message. It could even be seen as a paradigm (a sort of model example) for the punishment of a trilogy of sins: lechery (Nicholas); avarice (John) and pride (Absolon). In the end you have to weigh up in your mind whether you feel that such judgements are strongly asserted, or whether the element of comic farce makes them less likely.

As well as religion and spirituality, there is an associated theme of prediction which becomes important. It is sometimes referred to as the theme of 'prophecy'.

Activity

Look through the tale and identify points where the themes of prophecy and warning are part of the tale. Consider these themes as they relate to: Nicholas' astrology and the parody of Noah's flood.

Discussion

What you need to think about is the way that Nicholas appears so convincing in his prophecy, because of his interest in astrology. This, plus his conniving approach to the gullible John, lends him an air of great authority. It also flatters John, tailored as it is to the carpenter's belief in Old Testament stories. Like Noah, he could be a patriarchal hero with Alison and Nicholas by his side. Do you find it at all significant that the prophecy should be similar to Noah's flood? The biblical association seems important to me: the hoax is a grand one, absurd in the extreme. This adds to the mockery of John – how could anyone, we wonder, be quite so easily fooled by such an unlikely prediction? The mockery is compounded by the association between carpenters and the story of the flood.

Just before the prediction of the flood is made, there is another kind of prediction built into the structure of the tale. This is when John says that Nicholas *shal be rated of his studiyng* (355). At the time we could be forgiven for taking little notice of John's concern for the effects of scholarship. But in the end, has John got a point? Because we become diverted by the central comic prediction of the flood, are we in danger of missing the real prediction – the one that will come true when Nicholas takes his cleverness too far?

Other Possible Themes

Because of the structure of the tale, its elements of parody and the extremes of behaviour, there are other contrasting themes. There is not room here to discuss them in detail, but consider these: youth and age; learning and ignorance; love and hatred; work and pleasure.

Approaches through Poetic Technique

Style

You have already learnt a great deal about realism and the associated styles of animalism and naturalism in the tale. You have also read about the form of *fabliau* which allows the comedy and mockery to emerge so strongly.

Some aspects of the style of this tale have already been discussed. You need to look back at the section on Realism, pp. 93–6. Realism contributes a great deal. It is a style appropriate to the *mockery* of courtly romance. The Miller attempts to express how the characters live in a very basic and unromantic way – as a point of ironic contrast to the courtly characters in *The Knight's Tale*. The familiarity of events and the down-to-earth behaviour of the characters is contrasted with other styles of writing, and this mixture contributes to a magnificent parody.

Parody

Parody is imitation. Writers frequently use the form and style of another work or genre of literature in which to cast their own. Many writers have used parody in order to write in a mocking, satirical and humorous way. A modern term, (amongst other more colloquial terms) which would sum up parody would be a 'send-up'.

Many critics have recognized that, even though Chaucer tells a story of the worst kind of ribaldry set in a very realistic world, it is also a story about pretentions to courtly love. This mock-courtliness is especially strong in the descriptions of the characters of Nicholas, Alison and Absolon, as you have seen.

It is also evident in their dialogues with each other. For fear of being denied, Nicholas cries to Alison for mercy and tells her he will die without her love. Through an exaggerated dialogue, in which there appears to be terrible pain and anguish, Chaucer creates in the character of Nicholas a parody of the hero-lover. This also happens through his musical skills. We realize of course from his more direct sexually explicit actions (he pats her about the loins!) that he intends sex to be the goal of his courtliness with Alison. Nicholas is thus presented as both a courtier, and more directly, as a man of passion and lust. We can assume anyway that he is good at combining the two talents. We know this from the line: *Of deerne love he koude and of solas;* (92).

Courtly lovers worth their salt would have been good at secret love. Having seen elements of the courtly code in *hende* Nicholas, we then also see them in Absolon, although his courtliness is of a far less subtle nature. With Absolon, the parody of courtly behaviour is arguably stronger than in Nicholas. Throughout the long introduction to this rather flamboyant character, we get a picture of a young man trying to live almost entirely by a courtly code. The careful attention he pays to his clothing, its rather effeminate pinkish colour, his singing, dancing and musical playing, all give an impression of the courtly lover's code, and the mockery is then suggested by his squeamishness and also by the fact that he was *jolif...and gay* (231).

To continue with these three mock-courtly characters: if Nicholas' character reveals accomplishments and expresses the ultimate aim of sexual conquest in secret courtly love, and if Absolon is the essence of courtly jollity, then Alison seems to fit neatly into the category of desirable heroine. We know that she is desirable, but look at the technique used to describe her clothes. The clothing is deliberately presented in a sensual manner, particularly in the line which locates her apron: *Upon hir lendes, ful of many a goore.* (129). It is almost as if we can visualize her loins through the description of the clothing used to cover them.

It may be that Chaucer means us to be suspicious of Alison: she does seem to attract men easily and then The Miller tells us that nowhere is there *swich a wenche* (146). It has been suggested that there is a possible double meaning in the word *wenche*. It could simply mean that she is a servant girl, but the word can also suggest 'slut'. Certainly we know that she is quick to offer herself to Nicholas. This lack of reserve may be part of the parody. She is not only delicately beautiful but sexually very enticing too.

There is a recurring reference to music and other courtly pastimes. Nicholas played on his *gay sautrie* (105), so well that *all the chambre rong* (107). He also sang *The Angel to the Virgin Mary* and *The King's Tune* in a voice that was very accomplished. Absolon tries to exhibit the same quality of courtly behaviour with his playing and singing. He sings to Alison beneath her window, accompanied by the playing of his gittern. A few lines later we are given an attractive impression of his singing through the image of the nightingale: *He syngeth, brokkynge as a nyghtyngale;* (269). The courtliness of both these clerks is emphasized through their musical talents as well as their dress and appearance. The strongest mockery of courtliness is expressed in the lines which describe Absolon almost as a stereotype of the vain courtier (212 – 28). These lines should help you to build-up a picture of the expected behaviour of the courtier. What impressions of courtly behaviour do you receive from this description?

Moving from character to action, E.T. Donaldson in his essay, 'Idiom of Popular Poetry in *The Miller's Tale*' suggests that Chaucer parodies closely the structure and direction of a courtly love-story. The secret wooing would be motivated by a *love-longynge* (241), which Absolon suffers. He uses a traditional image of the turtle-dove to express the strength and pull of this longing, yet mocks it in a rather more cumbersome image: *'I moorne as dooth a lamb after the tete.'* (596).

A feature of medieval courtly romance would have been that, at some time during the story, a feast would be described. This could either be a literal feast – a meal, or a metaphorical feast – of love. Chaucer uses this idea to parody the courtly romance. During the adultery passage, there are a number of phrases which, it has been suggested, are there to mock the melody and harmony which is often part of the feast idea in medieval romances. John moans, groans and snores loudly in his sleep:

> For travaille of his goost he groneth soore,
> And eft he routeth, for his heed myslay.   (538–9)

When Nicholas and Alison descend the ladder, *Ther was the revel and the melodye.* (544).

Religious parody in the ecclesiastical sounds of the bells also adds to the sense of climax. These sounds should be sombre and religious, but here they seem to contribute to the indulgent and blissful state being enjoyed by the adulterers:

> And thus lith Alison and Nicholas,
> In bisynesse of myrthe and of solas,
> Til that the belle of laudes gan to rynge,
> And freres in the chauncel gonne synge.   (545–8)

Throughout this book, mention has been made of the comparisons between *The Miller's Tale* and *The Knight's Tale*. To remind you, the subject of *The Knight's Tale* is idealized love. This is love which is romantic, and the tone of the poem is elevated and slow, in accordance with the high ideals of courtly love. One of the ways in which *The Miller's Tale* parodies *The Knight's Tale* is through the stress on sexuality as opposed to ideal romantic love.

Activity

Choose some of the lines and phrases which show that *The Miller's Tale* is concerned more with sexuality in romance than it is with love.

Discussion.

It should not be difficult for you to pick out the key phrases which are overtly sexual. Do also think about the way that sexual drives dictate the behaviour of the characters. A courtly hero should have been willing to work hard at the wooing of his lady and have been patient enough to wait a long time for her to answer his advances. This ideal time span would have allowed for romance to flourish, and would have made the final consummation of their love all the more worth waiting for.

Consider again the elements of animalism in Alison. The description introduces her as if she were a more typical romantic courtly heroine, but because the description concentrates on the earthy side of nature, the stress is placed instead on her sexual drive rather than on the more traditional courtly qualities of romance.

Absolon, as we have seen, tries to be much more like a traditional courtly lover, but in view of the phobias he has and ultimately because he is such a failure, he proves that he cannot be a successful courtier. All we get with Absolon is the courtly code – he knows just what to say and do, but in the end there is no substance to him, and far from being a successful courtier, he comes across as excessively foolish. Can you see how this too is a way of parodying courtliness? Absolon's character undermines courtliness, not least when the courtly hero bites on Alison's bum at the very moment when he assumes he is going to enjoy a romantic kiss!

Nicholas is sexually very bold. Consider how forward and lacking in shame he is when we first see him attempt to seduce Alison. The charms of a courtly lover come second for him. First, he is eager to approach Alison directly:

> so bifel the cas
> That on a day this hende Nicholas
> Fil with this yonge wyf to rage and pleye, (163–5)

Later, when he finally goes to bed with her, there is no mistaking the pleasure they both gain from the experience (544–8). Nicholas is, by contrast to Absolon, a much more confident and successful man, at least until the tables are turned on him at the end. Yet the impression is not just of his sexual confidence; he is good at behaving like a wounded courtly lover in the way that he persuades Alison, and he is of course good at fooling others. This all contributes to the impression of a self-indulgent character who can win his way with the wife of another man.

Association

Chaucer tells his story economically so that the events of the narrative progress in a way that grip listener and reader. Yet, his sense of structure is acute. What you will find is that there are a number of associations which, on close analysis, relate to each other.

The more you look for associations and connections between one part of the story and another, the more possibilities you can find. In the first few lines of the tale we are given some insight, perhaps without our realizing it, into the main part of the plot. The introduction to Nicholas' astrology points to the main events of the story.

In the introduction to John there are further associations which then recur in other parts of the tale. There is discussion early in the poem of the problems concerning the marital age difference and this is then explored throughout the action of the tale: John proves to be a gullible old fool and Alison to be a lusty, energetic young adulterer.

The flirtatious early relations between Nicholas and Alison are a forerunner of the night of passion they are able to spend later with each other. Here Chaucer uses a style of provocative dialogue which is playful and scheming.

You have already read about how the series of ironic associations are developed during the night of adultery. It is one of Chaucer's finest passages. He cleverly constructs the action with a number of contrasts. Whilst John snores in his attic, his head lying awkwardly, Nicholas and Alison go to bed and we can only leave to our erotic imaginations exactly what Chaucer meant by the line *Ther was the revel and the melodye*; (544) used to describe their activity, in contrast to John's noisy slumbers.

Look also at the frequent mention of matters relating to Absolon's mouth. It itches for the desire of a kiss with Alison, he chews *greyne and lycorys, / To smellen sweete* (582–3) and then comes the fateful kiss; and notice how strongly he reacts to this:

> Who rubbeth now, who froteth now his lippes
> With dust, with sond, with straw, with clooth, with chippes, (639–40)

Throughout, there are associations connected with the medieval world of work, and work generally comes to play a part in the structure and development of the story. Carpenters were frequently the ones who put on the Mystery Play of Noah's Ark, and we see in the building of the tub just how successful John is at his work. It is presumably his work that takes him away from home in the first place. His response to Nicholas' fit is very practical and workmanlike: he gets Robyn to break down the door. Nicholas senses that a good way to appeal to John, – to make him, in effect, even more gullible, is to get him to associate work with hope: after being told about the coming flood, John asks rather ruefully: *'Is ther no remedie in this cas?'* (417), and Nicholas answers: *'If thou wolt werken after loore and reed.'* (419), and he goes on to quote Solomon from the *Bible*, about the saving of Noah. There is a lovely combination of styles here: the convincing but devious patter of Nicholas who has assessed John accurately as a character proud of his workmanship; and the sincerity of the poor duped John who will set to and use all his skills and tricks of the trade to build the *knedyng trogh* (440) as a means, like Noah, of saving himself and his family. By contrast, the styles of speech of the two clerks and the descriptions of how they spend their time reveal that they are men with little of any importance to do, except devise schemes, and play love games. In the end the world of work has a powerful role to play, overcoming the indolent and indulgent lives of the three courtly characters. The smith, Gerveys, is similar to John, and ultimately, without realizing it, connected with him. In the same way that John, ironically, has no problem solving the coming flood, so too Gerveys solves Absolon's problem. Unwittingly he hands over the perfect solution. He is an affable chap, and of course Absolon can have the iron blade – he'll just go and get it from the chimney – and Gerveys tactfully asks no questions as to why it is needed. The final meeting of hot blade on skin is like a climax of the conflict between two worlds – Nicholas' indolent world of jokes and patter; and a down-to-earth world of practical behaviour.

Activity

There are a number of other associations you might be able to find if you search the text closely enough. Look again, for example, at the way that nature is used. Consider how successfully Chaucer applies references to authoritative sources – to the *Bible*, to ancient philosophy, and to the science of astrology. Do you notice any others?

Discussion

The poem contains a variety of styles. Chaucer switches comfortably from moments of learned or biblical reference to images of nature, animals or the farmyard, which contributes to the comic parody. In the form of *fabliau,* he is able to set a story, full of powerful messages, within the very real world of ordinary people. Again, this is where comparison with *The Knight's Tale* is helpful. In that story, the real world never intervenes. *The Miller's Tale* is a mixed world, but in the end, by comparison with *The Knight's Tale*, it is about some extremely basic and earthily instinctive behaviour.

Consider also the relationship between *The Miller's Prologue* and the words spoken by Chaucer and The Reeve in *The Reeve's Prologue*. Chaucer's comment that the tale had mostly been received light-heartedly recalls his expressed anxiety in *The Miller's Prologue*. Perhaps his words in *The Reeve's Prologue* let him off the hook altogether, as after all it is only The Reeve himself who takes offence, and that is for a particular reason. If the other pilgrims have laughed, then why needed he to worry in the first place?

Imagery

As has been suggested, the style of imagery varies according to the character for whom it is used. Some of it contributes to the earthy quality of the poem, some of it to the courtly parody. As is the case with the proverbial sayings, much of the imagery often sounds conversational, and it is always worth listening to the tone used by each speaker as much as the poetic quality of the imagery itself. (This is as true of all the dialogue – not just the imagery.) The result is often considerable realism or parody. The point cannot be stressed often enough that this realistic, conversational imagery is drawn from wide and varied aspects of life. However, such versatility is not simply a display of Chaucer's knowledge. What the imagery seems to achieve is perhaps more profound: it is like a concentration of life forces which merge into one story. There are at times the forces of nature, sometimes drawn from the animal world, on other occasions a representation of the reality of human life, and at other times imagery intended to mock the foolish courtly and amorous aspirations of the characters, A close appreciation of the imagery suggests this combination of contrasting lifestyles: the mixing together of rural and courtly lives, the eloquent and the ordinary, nature and everyday human objects.

Activity
Consider the variety of images used in the tale. Which areas of experience are represented? Why do you think there are more similes than metaphors?

Discussion
The images all seem to be appropriate to the characters or events being described, in just the same way as a good raconteur draws on

experience to make his stories more vivid and lively. The other tonal effect is that the imagery can be quite stunning, even though it appears to be naturally part of conversation and story-telling, and of course it allows for a web of associations and sensations to be built-up around the characters.

The first few images surprise us. Nicholas was sly and secretive: *And lyk a mayden meke for to see.* (94). His attractiveness, which comes to provide such an appeal for Alison, is built around his sweet-smelling body by using an image from the natural world:

And he hymself as sweete as is the roote
Of lycorys, or any cetewale. (98–9)

There is a great deal of animal imagery associated with John, the choice of which seems entirely appropriate to his foolish and small-minded character: *Jalous he was, and heeld hire narwe in cage,* (116); and *But sith that he was fallen in the snare,* (123). These animal images fit naturally into the tone of chattiness in the descriptions of these ordinary people, and yet seem to work on another level – they come from a side of nature which is self-destructive and negative. Refer to the introductions of the other characters, especially the celebrated sensual characteristics of Alison.

At this point it is also worth referring back to the discussion of Proverbs, p. 120. As has been suggested, some of the imagery comes to sound like proverbial truth – on the one hand part of chatty discourse, but on the other hand, in a style which slows the poem down, implying thoughts of great and wise moment. Did you find this to be the case with line 468?:

'Thanne shaltou swymme as myrie, I undertake,
As dooth the white doke after hire drake.' (467–8)

or:

Derk was the nyght as pich, or as the cole, (623)

Is there a similar stark truth in the rather sad reflection on Absolon after he *hadde kist hir ers* (647). Cured of his *love-longynge* (241), he is destined to: *weep as dooth a child that is ybete.* (651).

As for the preponderance of simile over metaphor, think about the way that the longer use of similes allows for the realistic tone of speech from the story-teller to be maintained. In a sense, similes are more explanatory, perhaps even less 'poetic' than metaphors.

The Narrator's Voice

In *The Miller's Tale*, this realistic tone in the narrator's voice happens in other ways as well as through the use of imagery. The Miller is continually interrupting his own story to help him pace it and move it steadily along, for example:

Now, sire, and eft, sire, so bifel the cas	(163)
As clerkes ben ful subtile and ful queynte;	(167)
Now ber thee wel, thou hende Nicholas,	(289)

The purposes of the narrator's involvement can, however, be interpreted in different ways. Are we simply to see the technique as part of the structure of telling a good yarn, thereby keeping up the pace and maintaining the interest of the listener, or is the implication that the narrator wishes to apply a set of values to the meanings of the story?

This concluding point might bring you back to consider the question: is *The Miller's Tale* a story of moral truths or a bawdy farce? Can it be both? And finally, does *The Reeve's Prologue* help us find the answer to this question?

Chronology

1376–7	Further travelling in Flanders and France on King's secret business. In 1376 'Good Parliament' meets; death of Edward, the Black Prince. 1377 Death of Edward III; accession of Richard II
1378	Travelled again to Italy – renewed acquaintance with works of Italian writers
1378–80	*The House of Fame* written; 1379 Richard II introduces Poll Tax
1380–2	*The Parliament of Fowls*; 1381 Peasants' Revolt
1380s	Moved to Kent (precise date unknown)
1382–6	*Troilus and Criseyde* and *The Legend of Good Women* written; 1385 gave up the post at Customs House; became Justice of the Peace
1386	Gave up house at Aldgate; election to Parliament
1387	Phillipa presumed to have died
1388–92	The *General Prologue* and earlier *Canterbury Tales* written; 1389–91 appointed to be Clerk of the King's works. 1391–2 *A Treatise on the Astrolabe* written
1392–5	Most of *The Canterbury Tales* completed
1396–1400	Later *Canterbury Tales* written; 1396 Anglo-French Treaty. 1397–9 Richard II's reign of 'tyranny'
1399	Returned to London, in a house near The Lady Chapel of Westminster Abbey; deposition of Richard II; accession of Henry IV
1400	Chaucer died (date on tomb in Westminster Abbey given as 25 October)

Further Reading

Editions and Commentaries

The following books have useful notes, especially those by Winny and Brewer:

L. D. Benson (ed.), *The Riverside Chaucer* (Oxford University Press, 1988).

Elisabeth Brewer, *The Miller's Tale* (Longman, 1982) York Notes.

T. W. Ross (ed.), *'The Miller's Tale'* (Norman, 1983), Volume II, part 3 of *A Variorum Edition of the Works of Geoffrey Chaucer*.

W. W. Skeat (ed.), *The Complete Works*, Volume V (Oxford University Press, 1900).

James Winny (ed.), *The Miller's Prologue and Tale* (Cambridge University Press, 1971).

Biography

D. R. Howard, *Chaucer, His Life, His Works, His World* (Dutton, New York, 1987).

G. Kane, *Chaucer* (Past Masters Series) (Oxford University Press, 1984).

D. Pearsall, *The Life of Geoffrey Chaucer* (Blackwell, 1992).

Criticism

J. A. W. Bennett, *Chaucer at Oxford and Cambridge* (Oxford University Press, 1974).

This book contains two essays on *The Canterbury Tales*; one by Charles Muscatine, the other by Nevill Coghill:

D.S. Brewer (ed.), *Chaucer and Chaucerians* (Nelson, 1966).

This critical work prints and translates three analogues of *The Miller's Tale*:

W. F. Bryan and G. Dempster (eds.), *Sources and Analogues of Chaucer's Canterbury Tales* (Chicago, 1941).

This book is still valuable on particular issues, though some of its conclusions have been contested:
W. C. Curry, *Chaucer and the Medieval Sciences* (London, 1960).

This book, pp. 90–108, explains the place of *The Miller's Tale* in *The Canterbury Tales*:
Alfred David, *The Strumpet Muse* (Indiana, 1976).

This essay discusses The Miller's parodies of medieval love-poetry:
E. T. Donaldson, 'The Miller's Tale' A3483–6, first published in A. S. Downer (ed.), *English Institute Essays* 1950 (Columbia, 1951). It has been reprinted many times, notably in Donaldson's, *Speaking of Chaucer* (Athlone, 1970).

This critical work brings Charles Muscatine's account of the *fabliau* up-to-date:
J. Hines, *The Fabliau in English* (London, 1993).

This book discusses the action of the first five *Canterbury Tales* in the light of contemporary visual materials:
V. A. Kolve, *Chaucer and the Imagery of Narrative* (London, 1984).

This is still the best book on Chaucer and contains an interesting discussion of *fabliau* (pp. 58–71). You will also find a very influencial chapter on the style of *The Miller's Tale* (pp. 223–30):
Charles Muscatine, *Chaucer and the French Tradition* (California, 1957).

This book, pp. 166–83, provides an excellent critical account of the issues in the tale:
D. Pearsall, *The Canterbury Tales* (Unwin, 1985).

This book contains a helpful essay on *fabiau* tales – 'The *Fabliaux*' by D. S. Brewer:
Beryl Rowland (ed.), *Companion to Chaucer Studies* (Oxford University Press, 1968).

Language

D. Burnley, *A Guide to Chaucer's Language* (Methuen, London, 1983).
N. Davis (ed.), *A Chaucer Glossary* (Oxford University Press, 1968).

Tasks

1 How is humour in the tale brought out?

2 Write about one of the main characters in detail to explain:
   - the effect of the introduction to the character;
   - his or her development through the plot;
   - the destiny of the character in the tale.

3 Do you agree that John is a fool?

4 How clever is Nicholas?

5 In what ways is the characterization of Alison a parody of the courtly heroine? How does she differ from a more typical courtly heroine?

6 Do you sympathize with Absolon?

7 Do you consider the suffering endured by Absolon and Nicholas to be just?

8 To what extent does the tale depend on a mixture of styles for its success?

9 Consider the techniques used by Chaucer to establish aspects of the real medieval world in the story.

10 How important is the contrast between old age and youth in the tale?

11 Whatever its meanings or values, there is no doubt that *The Miller's Tale* is one of the most entertaining of all the stories in *The Canterbury Tales*. Which parts of the story do you find most entertaining, and what makes them so?

12 From your understanding of The Miller in the portrait in the *General Prologue*, does the tale appear to express his character?

13 Which scenes strike you as dramatically effective?

14 Defend the tale against the charge that it should not be taught in schools because of its bawdy subject matter.

15 Why is it so important to read *The Miller's Prologue* and *The Reeve's Prologue* in addition to *The Miller's Tale*?

A portrait of Chaucer from the presentation copy of Hoccleve's *The Regement of Princes*. produced in the 1410s. Hoccleve's text suggests that this is an accurate image of Chaucer painted just a few years after his death

The Miller and The Reeve: two marginal illustrations from the Ellesmere manuscript. Compare with the description of The Miller on p. 1

A fourteenth-century English astrolabe, used to measure the position of the planets, like the one owned by Nicholas, see line 101

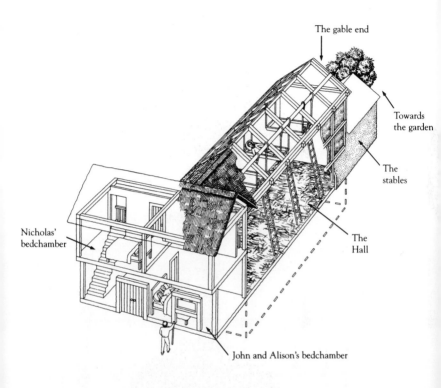

The gable end

Towards
the garden

The
stables

Nicholas'
bedchamber

The
Hall

John and Alison's bedchamber

A reconstruction of John the Carpenter's house based on the descriptions in the
The Miller's Tale

The Devil and Mrs Noah: Noah building the ark (below) with a devil tempting Noah's wife to obstruct him (above). The image is from *Queen Mary's Psalter*, an East Anglian manuscript of 1310-1320 illustrating the traditional story of Noah's wife hindering the progress of the ark, as Nicholas relates it in lines 426-54

A Note on Chaucer's English

Chaucer's English has so many similarities with Modern English that it is unnecessary to learn extensive tables of grammar. With a little practice, and using the glosses provided, it should not be too difficult to read the text. Nevertheless, it would be foolish to pretend that there are no differences. The remarks which follow offer some information, hints and principles to assist students who are reading Chaucer's writings for the first time, and to illustrate some of the differences (and some of the similarities) between Middle and Modern English. More comprehensive and systematic treatments of this topic are available in *The Riverside Chaucer* and in D. Burnley, *A Guide to Chaucer's Language*.

1 Inflections

These are changes or additions to words, usually endings, which provide information about number (whether a verb or a noun is singular or plural) tense or gender.

a) *Verbs*

In the **present** tense most verbs add –e in the first person singular (e.g. *I ryde*), –est in the second person singular (e.g. *thou sayest*), –eth in the third person singular (*she sayeth*) and –en in the plural. This can be summarized as follows:

	Middle English	Modern English
Singular	1 I telle	I tell
	2 Thou tellest	You tell
	3 He/She/It telleth	He/She/It tells
Plural	1 We tellen	We tell
	2 Ye tellen	You tell
	3 They tellen	They tell

As you can see, Middle English retains more inflections than Modern English, but the system is simple enough. Old English, the phase of the language between around 449 AD, when the Angles first came to Britain, and about 1100, had many more inflections.

In describing the **past** tense it is necessary to begin by making a distinction, which still applies in Modern English, between strong and weak verbs. **Strong verbs** form their past tense by changing their stem (e.g. I sing, I sang; you drink, you drank; he fights, he fought; we throw, we threw), while **weak verbs** add to the stem (I want, I wanted; you laugh, you laughed; he dives, he dived).

In the past tense in Middle English, strong verbs change their stems (e.g. *sing* becomes *sang* or *song*) and add –e in the second person singular (e.g. *thou songe*) and –en in the plural (e.g. *they songen*). Weak verbs add –de or –te (e.g. *fele* becomes *felte*, *here* becomes *herde*) with –st in the second person singular (e.g. *thou herdest*) and –n in the plural (e.g. *they felten*). The table below compares the past tense in Middle and Modern English for strong and weak verbs.

Strong Verbs

	Middle English Present stem: 'sing'	**Modern English**
Singular	1 I sange (or soonge)	I sang (or sung)
	2 Thou songe	You sang
	3 He/She/It sange	He/She/It sang
Plural	1 We songen	We sang
	2 Ye songen	You sang
	3 They songen	They sang

Weak Verbs

	Middle English Present stem: 'here'	**Modern English** hear
Singular	1 I herde	I heard
	2 Thou herdest	You heard
	3 He/She/It herde	He/She/It heard
Plural	1 We herden	We heard
	2 Ye herden	You heard
	3 They herden	They heard

The past tense can also be formed using the auxiliary verb *Gan* plus the past participle (e.g. *gan... dresse* [360]: went, *gan wype* [622]: wiped). *Gan* sometimes means 'began' in phrases involving the preposition 'to' (e.g. *gan to rynge* [547]: began to ring) but even in some of these cases past tense is required (e.g. *gan to stele* [678]: stole, went). Some verbs add initial *y* to make their past participle (e.g. *ytoold* [1]: told, *ydight* [97]: adorned).

b) Nouns and Adjectives

Nouns mostly add –s or –es for plural (e.g. *songes* [223]) and possessive (e.g. *wrightes* [35], but notice *carpenteris* [235], *carpenteres* [248]). There are no apostrophes in Middle English! (But modern editors sometimes add one to indicate that a letter has been elided, e.g. *M'athynketh* [62]). Some nouns add –en for plural (e.g. *eyen* [209]). Although (unlike modern French or German) nouns do not take grammatical gender in Middle English, some nouns add –e for feminine (e.g. *tappestere* barmaid [228]. Some adjectives add –e in plural. Some adjectives are converted to adverbs by the addition of –e (e.g. *faire* [181]: graciously).

c) Personal Pronouns

The forms of the personal pronouns are somewhat different from those used in Modern English and are worth recording in full:

			Subject	Object	Possessive
Singular	1		I, ich	me	myn, my
	2		Thou, thow	thee	thyn, thy
	3	masculine	He	hym, him	his
	3	feminine	She	her	hir, hire
	3	neuter	It, hit	it, hit	his
Plural	1		We	us	owre, our, owres
	2		Ye	you, yow	your, youres
	3		They	hem	hire, here

Remember that the distinction between *thou* and *you* in Middle English often involves politeness and social relationship as well as number. This is similar to modern French or German. Thus *thou* forms are used with friends, family and social inferiors, *you* forms with strangers or superiors. There are occasions when changes between the forms seem to indicate a change in the speaker's attitude to the person addressed (as in Absolon's speeches at the window [590–681, 684–97]), but in other places it is hard to detect any significance in the change (e.g. 176–79).

2 Relative Pronouns

The main **relative pronouns** found are *that* and *which*. In translating *that* it is often wise to try out a range of Modern English equivalents, such as *who*, *whom*, *which*. The prefix *ther-* in such words as *therto* and *therwith* often refers back to the subject matter of the previous phrase. *Therto* may be translated as 'in addition to all that' or 'in order to achieve that'.

3 Impersonal Construction

With certain verbs the **impersonal construction** is quite common (e.g. *hym leste* [313]: it pleased him, *Me reweth* [354]: it saddens me, *M' athynketh* [62]: it seems to me, *nedeth nat enquere* [58]: there is no need to ask).

4 Reflexive Pronouns

Many verbs can be used with a **reflexive pronoun**, a pronoun which refers back to the subject (as in modern French or German) and which may, depending on the verb employed, be translated or understood as part of the verb (e.g. *dressed hym* [250]: placed himself, *shapen hym* [295]: devise, *blessen hym* [340]: cross himself).

5 Extra Negatives

In Middle English extra **negatives** often make the negative stronger, whereas in Modern English double negatives cancel each other out. *Ther nys no man* (145) would now be 'there is no man', *I nam no labbe* (401) 'I am no tell-tale'. Lines 309-10 present a more complicated case.

> For, for no cry hir mayde koude hym calle,
> He nolde answere for thyng that myghte falle.

This means 'in spite of any cry her maid could make to him, he would not answer, whatever happened.'

6 Contraction

Sometimes negatives and pronouns merge with their associated verbs (e.g. *noot* [= *ne woot*] [556]: did not know, *knowestow* [48]: do you know, *artow* [49]: are you).

7 Word Order

Middle English **word order** is often freer than Modern English, and in particular there is more inversion of subject and verb (e.g. *Crul was his heer* [206]) or subject and object (e.g. *A brooch she baar* [157]). In analysing difficult sentences you should first locate the verb, then its subject, then the object or complement. (Roughly, a verb which involves activity takes an object – she hit the ball, he gave her the book – while a verb which describes a state of affairs takes a complement – it was yellow, you look better.) Then you should put these elements together. It should then be easier to see how the various qualifiers fit in.

In the sentence beginning at line 433, the main verbs are 'be' and 'hadde had'. By putting them together with their subjects and complements we reach 'he had rather that she had had a ship'. Then we can find places for the qualifiers: 'I dare well say that at that time **he would rather** than all his black male sheep **that she had had a ship** for herself alone.'

Chaucer sometimes adds to his sentences in ways that you might be criticized for. For example the second sentence of the tale keeps elaborating on Nicholas' skill at astrology and the kinds of questions people might ask him, until the poet gives up on the sentence: 'With him was living a poor scholar, who had studied arts but preferred to concentrate on astrology, and knew some of the propositions such as how to determine by looking at the stars, if men should ask him, whether it would rain or be dry at a certain time, or if they asked him what should happen in some other matter; I cannot recount all possible cases.' Any modern English teacher would make three or four sentences out of this, but perhaps Chaucer achieves an effect by allowing the sentence to meander on.

Extra qualifications can make short sentences harder to unravel. In the sentence beginning at line 642, the main idea (in lines 643-44) is fairly easy to grasp: 'I would rather than all this town that I should be avenged for this insult.' But the addition of another expression complicates the idea: 'May I give my soul to Satan if I would not rather than all this town be avenged for this insult.'

8 Connection of Clauses

Middle English often does not indicate **connection of clauses** as clearly as Modern English. In seeking to understand or in translating you may need to provide connecting words (as I did in the discussion of the second sentence of the tale on p. 149). On occasion you may have to provide verbs which have been omitted (particularly the verb 'to be', e.g. *Hir filet brood of silk* [135]: Her broad headband was made of silk, or verbs of motion) or regularize number or tense (in some Middle English sentences a subject can shift from singular to plural or a verb from present to past).

Chaucer can mix the past tense with the historic present (sometimes in telling a story we use the present tense, even though we and our audience know that the events occurred in the past) but a Modern English writer would have to maintain consistency at least within the sentence and usually within the paragraph as well. Chaucer's usage here (and with the implied words and the lack of connectives) may well be closer to spoken English than modern formal writing could be.

9 Change of Meaning

Although most of the words which Chaucer uses are still current (often with different spellings) in Modern English, some of them have changed their meaning. (All the words in the first sentence of *The Miller's Prologue* exist in Modern English, but the modern meanings of *namely*, *route* [=rout] and *gentil* [=gentle] would be inappropriate here). So it is a good idea to check the Notes or the Glossary even for words which look familiar. If you are interested in investigating the ways in which words change their meanings over time you can look at the quotations provided in large historical dictionaries, such as the *Oxford English Dictionary* or the *Shorter Oxford Dictionary* or in R. W. Burchfield, *The English Language* (Oxford, 1985), pp.113-23, or G. Hughes, *Words in Time: A Social History of English Vocabulary* (Oxford, Blackwell). Here are some more examples from *The Miller's Tale*:

Middle English word	(line no.)	Meaning	Equivalent modern word
barge	(442)	ship, sea-going vessel	barge
cast	(497)	trick	cast
celle	(714)	floor	cell
chambre	(95)	bedroom	chamber
cheere	(510)	expression	cheer
child	(217)	young man, lad	child
chippes	(640)	woodchips	chips
clerk	(91)	student, learned man	clerk
conseil	(395, 422)	secret, advice	counsel
daungerous	(230)	fastidious	dangerous
deffie	(650)	denounce	defy
drenchen	(509)	drown	drench
estaat	(121)	position in society, status	estate, state
filet	(135)	headband	fillet
fyndyng	(112)	provision, gifts	findings
gentil	(63)	noble, highborn, virtuous	gentle

A Note on Pronunciation

The Miller's Tale, like other poems, benefits from being read aloud. Even if you read it aloud in a Modern English pronunciation you will get more from it, but Middle English was pronounced differently (the sounds of a language change over time at least as much as the vocabulary or the constructions) and it helps to make some attempt at a Middle English accent. The best way to learn this is to imitate one of the recordings (the tapes issued by Pavilion and Argo are especially recommended for this purpose). A few principles are given below, more can be found in *The Riverside Chaucer*.

1 In most cases you should pronounce all consonants (for example you should sound the 'k' in knight and the 'l' in half). But in words of French origin initial 'h' (as in *hostelrye* [95] for example) should not be sounded, nor should 'g' in the combination 'gn'. The combination 'gh' (as in *droghte* [88]) is best sounded 'ch' as in Scottish 'loch'.

2 In most cases all vowels are sounded, though a final 'e' may be silent because of elision with a vowel following (e.g. do not sound the second 'e' in *seyde it* [3]) or because of the stress pattern of the line (e.g. I would sound the final 'e' in *quite* [11], but leave it silent in *Millere* [12]).

3 Two points of spelling affect pronunciation. When 'y' appears as a vowel you should sound it as 'i' (see table on p. 153). Sometimes a 'u' sound before 'n' or 'm' was written 'o' (because 'u' and 'n' looked very similar in the handwriting of the time). This means that *song* and *yong* should be pronounced 'sung' and 'yung'. This also applies in *comen* and *sonne* (as in their Modern English equivalents 'come' and 'son').

4 You will not go too far wrong with combinations of vowels, such as *ai*, *eu* and *oy* if you sound them as in Modern English. There are significant exceptions (for example *mous* [238] and *hous* [248] and many words of similar ending should be pronounced with an *oo* sound) but it is not possible to establish reliable rules purely on the basis of the spelling.

5 The principal vowel sounds differ somewhat from Modern English. They are set out in the table below (adapted from Norman Davis' table in *The Riverside Chaucer*). The table distinguishes long and short versions of each vowel. This distinction still applies in Modern English (consider the 'a' sounds in hat and father) but unfortunately it is often only possible to decide whether a particular vowel is long or short by knowing about the derivation of the word. Do not despair. Even a rough approximation will help you. Only experts in medieval languages have reliable Middle English accents, and even they cannot be sure that Chaucer would have approved them.

Vowel	Middle English example	Modern equivalent sound
Long 'a'	cas (163), stable (464)	'a' in father
Short 'a'	sat (13), nat (24)	'a' in hat
Long 'e'	he (3), been (46)	'a' in fate
Open 'e'	heeth (154), teche (491)	'e' in there
Short 'e'	gent (126), wende (585)	'e' in set
Unstressed 'e'	nones (18), sonne (314)	'a' in about, 'e' in forgotten
Long 'i'	I (6), tyme (111)	'i' in machine
Short 'i'	hym (82), aright (7)	'i' in sit
Long 'o'	no (15), moot (6)	'o' in note
Open 'o'	hooly (400), goon (445)	'oa' in broad
Short 'o'	som (344), solas (92)	'o' in hot
Long 'u'	doute (453), mous (238)	'oo' in boot
Short 'u'	But (29), ful (46)	'u' in put

Glossary

This glossary is not absolutely comprehensive. It does not record all inflected forms (see A Note on Chaucer's English p. 145) nor all variant spellings. If you do not find a word here, try sounding it out, or try minor modifications of spelling (such as 'i' for 'y', 'a' for 'o', 'ea' for 'ee', and vice versa). Generally the main meaning in this text comes first, while more specialized meanings are given line references. Proper names which are explained in the Notes do not appear in the glossary. In compiling this glossary I have relied on L. D. Benson (ed.), *The Riverside Chaucer* and on N. Davis (ed.), *A Chaucer Glossary*, which offer fuller explanations than I can here. I have also consulted the *Oxford English Dictionary* and *The Middle English Dictionary*.

aboute around
abyd wait
abyde defer to (15)
accorded agreed
acordaunt in harmony with
acquitance release of property
adrad afraid
affeccioun love, emotion
after according to (112), about (554)
agast afraid
agayn again, towards, back
al all, entirely
Almageste astronomy textbook (see Notes p. 42, line 100)
also as
amydde in the middle of
amys wrongly
anon at once
a-nyghtes at night
apart apart, on their own
ape fool
apeyren injure
aright well
arraieth dresses
array condition, preparation
art the arts course (see Notes p. 40, line 83), astronomy (101)

art are
artow are you
aslake slacken, diminish, go down
astrelabie astrolabe
astrologye astrology (see Notes p. 40, line 84)
astromye astronomy
aswowne in a faint, unconscious
athynketh it displeases
atones at once
atwo in two, apart
atwynne apart
augrym stones, counting stones
availleth benefits, profits
avalen take off
avyseth consider
awook awoke
axed asked
ay always
ayens against, compared with

bad advised, commanded, told
balkes beams
barge boat, ship
barmclooth apron
barred striped
benedicitee bless
bent curved, arched
berne barn

bet better
biddeth prays, requests
bifalle happen
bifel happened
bifoore in front
biforn before
bigonne began
bigyle deceive
bileve creed
biseche ask
biset employ, bestow, place
bisynesse occupation, activity
bitake commend
blake black
blisful delightful
bokeler small shield
boldely confidently, immediately (325)
boos boss
bord board, stay
bord plank
bour bedroom
bragot bragget (an alcoholic drink made by fermenting ale and honey)
brawn muscle
brest breast, chest
brewhous pub
brocage use of an agent
brokkynge warbling, trilling
brood wide
brosten broken
broyden embroidered
bryd bird
bukke buck, male deer
but if unless

caped stared
capyng staring
care trouble
carl rogue
cas event, occurrence, situation, chance
cast trick
casten leap, fling
Catoun *Cato* (elementary reader)
celle floor
certes certainly

certeyn certain, some, exact, a particular
cetewale setwall, zedoary (a spice resembling ginger)
ceynt belt
chambre bedroom
chartre charter, legal document
chauncel chancel
chaunteth sings
cheere expression, appearance
cherl churl, rascal
chese choose
child lad
chippes woodchips
chymenee fireplace, hearth
clappe chatter
cleped called
clerk student, learned man (see Notes p. 41, line 91, p. 51, line 204)
clippe cut
cloisterer monk
clom quiet, silent
clomben climbed
cokewold cuckold, betrayed husband
col-black black, coalblack
cole coal
coler collar
comandement command, disposal
compaignye company, companions
conclusiouns propositions
conseil secret, advice (422)
cop top
corde rope
cors body, corpse
corven cut out
couched placed
cride shouted
crouche make the sign of the cross
crul curly
curteisie courtesy

dame mother
daun master
debaat quarrel, argument
dede dead
deede action

deel part
deere precious
deerelyng darling
deerne secret
defame defame, spoil someone's reputation
deffie denounce
demen judge, decide, believe, think
depe deeply
devel devil
devocioun devotion, prayer
deye die
disporte enjoy
doke duck
doute doubt, fear
drawen to impress on (4)
drenche drown
dresse prepare, put on clothes, direct attention to (360)
dressed placed (250)
dreynt drowned, submerged
droghte drought, dry weather
dronke drunk, drunken
dronken being drunk
drough drew
drow drew

echon each one, all
eek also, moreover (448)
eft again
eftsoones immediately, another time
eir air
elde old age
elles, ellis else, otherwise
elves evil spirits
enquere ask, investigate
entente intention, purpose
er before
ernest serious, seriousness
ers arse
erys ears
esily easily, gently
espye see, notice
estaat position in society, status
evere ever, always
everichon everyone, all of them
everideel every part, all of it
eyle ail, be wrong with

fair beautiful
faire beautifully, neatly (102), properly (460)
faldyng coarse woollen cloth
falsen falsify
fantasye imagination, desire, delusion
faste rapidly, vigorously, hard, securely (391)
fecche fetch
felaweshipe companions
fer far
ferde fared, acted, did
ferre farther
fetisly handsomely, elegantly
fey faith, honour
fil happened, began
filet headband
fle fly
foo foe, enemy
foond found, tried
for because of (12), in spite of, out of respect for (60)
forbere restrain
forlore utterly lost, damned
foyson plenty
freres friars
froteth rubs, chafes
ful very
fyndyng provision, gifts

gabbe talk excessively
game play, joke
gan was
gan to began to
gauren stare
gay elegant, delightful, bright, fine
gaylard lively
gent delicate
gentil noble, fine
gentillesse noble behaviour (see Notes p. 37, line 63)
gentils those of noble birth
gesse imagine, suppose
gestes lodgers
giterne gittern, stringed instrument (see Notes p. 52, line 225)
gleede embers

gnof churl, lout
goliardeys buffoon, joker
gon go, prosper (6)
goore fold, flounce
goost spirit, soul
gooth goes
grace mercy, forgiveness
gracious pleasing, attractive
grange granary, farm building
greet, grete great, large, long
greyn cardamom seed
gyternynge gittern-playing

haaf heaved
haliday holy day
halves sides
harlotrye crude stories, ribald talk
harm injury, wrong
harre hinges
harwed harrowed, plundered
haspe fastenings, hinges
hastif urgent
haunchebones thighs
heed head, mind, thoughts (420)
heeld kept
heeled healed
heeng hung
heer hair
heeste command
heeth heather
hem them
hende courteous, handy (see Notes p. 41, line 91)
hente seize, pounce
herestow do you hear?
herkneth listen
herneys equipment, clothing
herte heart
herys hairs
heve raise, lift
hewe colouring, complexion
hidous dreadful
hir, hire their
hir, hire her
hoolynesse holiness
hoor grey-haired
hoord store

hooste host
hoot hot
hopen dance
hors horse
hoses stockings
hostelrye lodging-house, large house, inn
hust hush, be quiet
hye high

icched itched
ich I
ilke same
impressioun impression (see Notes p. 70, lines 503-05)
in house (especially lodging-house)
inquisityf inquisitive, curious
interrogaciouns questions

jalous jealous
janglere chatterer, teller of tales
jape joke
jolif, joly pretty, high-spirited, frisky, lively, full of desire (247)
jubbe jug

kan know
kembeth combs
kers cress
kiked stared
kirtel tunic
knarre rugged man
knave servant
knedyng kneading
knowestow you know
konne know how to
koude understood
kymelyn kimlin, trough (see Notes p. 66, line 440)

labbe tell-tale, chatterbox
lat let
lat be stop, give up
latoun latten, brass
laudes lauds
leef page
leeste least
leet left, stopped
leeve, leve dear, beloved (285)

157

legende story, biography
leggen lay
lemman love, darling
lendes loins
lene lend
lese lose
leste pleased
levere rather, dearer
lewed ignorant, lascivious
leyser opportunity
lief dear
light cheerful, glad.
lightnesse agility
lik like
likerous lustful, delightful, attractive
list wish
lith lie
litherly badly
longynge belonging (101)
loore learning
lorn lost, destroyed
loth disliked
lough laughed
love-longynge passionate desire
lovely loving
lycorys liquorice
lyf life, biography, life story of a saint (33)

madde go mad (48, 451)
maistrye skill
maladye sickness
male bag
manere manner(s), way, kind of (573)
marle-pit clay pit
mateere subject-matter
mayden virgin (of either sex)
meede reward, money
meenes intermediaries, middlemen
meeth mead
meke gentle, submissive
merveyle wonder
mete food
mette dreamed
mislay lay wrongly

mo more
mooder mother
moorne mourn
moot might, may, must
moralitee moral teaching
morne morning
mowe may
mowled gone mouldy
mullok rubbish
myrie tuneful, happy
mysspeke say anything wrong

nam am not
namely especially
narwe closely (116)
nas was not
nat not
ne not, nor
nede need, necessity
nedeth it is necessary
newe new, recently (113)
noble coin (worth one third of a pound sterling) (148)
noght not, nothing
nolde would not, do not want
nones occasion
noon none, not one
noot do not know
nosethirles nostrils
nye near-by
nyght-spel night charm (see Notes p. 62, line 372)
nys is not
nyste did not know

o one
offrynge offering
oon one
ooth oath
ordinance command

paas pace
paramours love, lovemaking, lovers
pardee by God, certainly
parfay by my faith
passeth continues
passioun suffering (especially the suffering of Christ on the cross)

Pater-noster (Latin) 'Our Father', *The Lord's Prayer*
pere-jonette early ripening pear
perled decorated with beads
pich pitch
piggesnye pig's eye (a flower)
pipyng whistling
pleye frolic, amuse oneself, joke (see Notes p. 74, line 578)
plogh plough, ploughteam (51)
poke bag
popelote pet, little doll
poure poor
poynt-devys carefully, to the last detail
poyntes laces
preche preach
presse cupboard
preye beg, ask
privee discreet, secretive
prively secretly
profred offered
propre beautiful
proprely neatly
protestacioun solemn declaration
prye observe
pryme about nine a.m.
prymerole primrose
pryvetee secrets, private parts (see Notes p. 35, line 56)
purveiance preparations, foresight
pyment spiced wine

quake tremble
queynte sly (167), elegant, pleasing thing (see Notes p. 48, line 168), elaborate (497)
quite, quyte reply to, repay, rival
quod said
quynyble high treble

rage sport (with a sexual sense)
rated scolded
rathe early
raughte reached
reed red
reed advice (419)
reherce relate, repeat

rekene count
remenant rest
rente income
reve reeve, estate-manager
revel merriment
rewe take pity
rist rose
roghte care
rometh roams, makes his way
ronges rungs
route, rowte company
routeth snores
rubible rebec, a small two-stringed fiddle
rude uneducated, ignorant
rys bough

saugh saw
sautrie psaltery (a stringed instrument)
scaffold platform
scape escape
scole school, style
scoler scholar
se see
seken seek
sely simple, unfortunate, foolish
sencer censer (vessel containing incense)
sensynge spreading incense
sermonyng preaching
sette sit, place
seye say, mean (497)
seyde said
seyl sail
seyn say
seystow do you say
shapen devise, form
shette shut, locked
shilde forbid
shode parting (of hair)
shoon shone
shot-wyndowe hinged window (see Notes p. 54, line 250)
shour shower, rain
sik sigh
sikerly, sikirly certainly, indeed
simylitude likeness

159

sith since
sleigh sly, cunning
sloo sloe-berry
slye crafty
smal small, short, slender (126), delicately (212), high-pitched (252)
smale finely
smert pain
smok shift, slip
smoot struck
smyth blacksmith
smythed made, repaired
so as long as, provided that
softe discreetly, quietly
solas pleasure, delight, entertainment
somdeel somewhat
somwhat something
sond sand
song sung
soore bitterly, sorely
sooth truth
soothly truly
sorwe sorrow, trouble
soster sister
soun sound
Southwerk Southwark
sowne play, sound
spak spoke
spak agayn replied
speed hurry, succeed
spille die
spitously loudly, vehemently
sproong leaped, sprang
sprynge break (566)
squaymous squeamish
stalkes uprights
stalketh creeps
stant stands
stele handle (677)
stele creep (678)
sterte awoke, leaped
stille quietly, silent
stirynge moving
stondeth stands
stoon stone

storial historical
stree straw
stroke, strook blow
strouted spread out
sturdily resolutely, boldly
stynt stop
suffisant enough
suffiseth be satisfied
surplys robe
suyte pattern
swalwe swallow
swelte melt
swete sweat (594)
swich such
swogh groan
swoote sweet
swymme float
swynke labour, toil
syn since

tale story, words, talk
tapes ribbons
tappestere barmaid
tarie remain, delay
tariying delay
tasseled adorned with tassels
teche teach
tete teat
thakked patted
thenche think, imagine
ther there, where
therto in addition, for that purpose
therupon on top of it
therwithal besides, also, at that (260)
thikke thickly, sturdy
thilke that same
tho at that time, then
tho those
thonder-dent thunderclap
thresshfold threshold
thriftily properly, fittingly
throte throat
thy your
tikel unstable
til to
toucheth concerns, treats
tour tower

toute, towte buttocks
tow flax
travaille suffering
trave frame for horses
trewe true, wise (421), faithful (501)
trewe-love herb paris (584)
trewely truly
trippe dance
trogh trough
trouthe troth, pledged word
trowe think, believe
turned directed
turtel turtle-dove
tweye two

unbokeled unbuckled, opened
underspore lever (from below)
undertake promise
unnethe hardly
until to (653)
untold uncounted

vengeaunce punishment, revenge
verraily truly
verray true
viritoot (see Notes p. 79, line 662)
vitaille victuals, food and drink
voluper cap

wafres cakes
waget sky-blue
wake stay up, remain awake
walwynge rolling, surging
war aware
warante swear, wager.
wayte watch, watch for, await
weel well
wel well, much
wenche lower-class woman, woman of loose morals, womanservant (523)
wende thought
wentestow did you go?
werede wore
werken act
werkes works, deeds
werte wart

wether male sheep
wey way
wey name (26)
weylawey alas
wezele weasel
whan when
whilom once
whit white
whoso whoever
wight creature, person
wille will, desires
wirche perform, do, work
wiste knew
wit reason, mind
wite know
withinne inside
withoute outside
wo sorrow, sadness, pain
wol will
wolle wool
wont accustomed
wood mad
woodnesse madness
woot know
woweth woos
wreye betray
wright carpenter
wrooth angry
wryed twisted
wyf woman, wife
wyle trick, stratagem
wynsynge skittish, lively
wyte blame

yaf gave
ybete beaten
yblent blinded
yborn carried
yclad dressed
ycleped called
ycrowe crowed
ydight decorated, arranged
ye eye (136)
ye you
yeman yeoman, free-born man
yerne lively
yeve give

yforged made, minted
ygeten got, obtained
ygrave engraved
yheere hear, heard
yleyd stowed away
ymaginacioun imagination
ynogh, ynowe enough
yong young

yoore formerly, long ago
yow you
ypulled plucked
yqueynt quenched
ysworn sworn
ytoold told
yvel evil, badly
ywis indeed

Appendix

The Description of The Clerk

Compare this description from the *General Prologue* with The Miller's description of Nicholas (91–112). How are the two descriptions organized? What are the differences between the two students? The comparison can reflect both the literary traditions of describing students (explored by Jill Mann in her *Chaucer and Medieval Estates Satire*), and the links between the pilgrim audience and the stories they hear.

> 285 A CLERK ther was of Oxenford also,
> That unto logyk hadde longe ygo.
> As leene was his hors as is a rake,
> And he nas nat right fat, I undertake,
> But looked holwe, and therto sobrely.
> 290 Ful thredbare was his overeste courtepy,
> For he hadde geten hym yet no benefice,
> Ne was so worldly for to have office.
> For hym was levere have at his beddes heed
> Twenty bookes, clad in blak or reed,
> 295 Of Aristotle and his philosophie
> Than robes riche, or fithele, or gay sautrie.
> But al be that he was a philosophre,
> Yet hadde he but litel gold in cofre;
> But al that he myghte of his freendes hente,
> 300 On bookes and on lernynge he it spente,
> And bisily gan for the soules preye
> Of hem that yaf hym wherwith to scoleye.
> Of studie took he moost cure and moost heede.
> Noght o word spak he moore than was neede,
> 305 And that was seyd in forme and reverence,
> And short and quyk and ful of hy sentence;
> Sownynge in moral vertu was his speche,
> And gladly wolde he lerne and gladly teche.

General Prologue 285–308

290 **overeste courtepy** short overcoat   291 **benefice** job in
the church   296 **fithele** a fiddle   297–8 The joke depends
on the fact that 'philosopher' could mean 'alchemist, one who devotes
himself to making gold'.   299 **hente** receive   302 **scoleye**
attend university   303 **cure** care   307 **Sownynge** in accord
with

The Description of the Courtly Lady

This is an example of the detailed description of a courtly lady,
parodied by Chaucer in his description of Alison (125–62). Notice
the detailed part by part description and the comparison with
valuable or courtly objects. This example is the description of
Idleness from Chaucer's translation of the *Roman de la Rose*
(539–61), a thirteenth century French poem describing the whole art
of love, written by Guillaume de Lorris and Jean de Meun. The
medieval manuals of poetry provided instructions for producing this
type of description (for example, Geoffrey de Vinsauf, *Poetria nova*,
562–99) and Chaucer provides another fine example in his youthful
work *The Book of the Duchess*, 817–1041.

Hir heer was as yelowe of hewe
540 As ony basyn scoured newe,
Hir flesh tendre as is a chike,
With bente browis smothe and slyke.
And by mesure large were
The openyng of hir yen clere,
545 Hir nose of good proporcioun,
Hir yen grey as is a faucoun,
With swete breth and wel savoured,
Hir face whit and wel coloured,
With litel mouth and round to see.
550 A clove chynne eke hadde she.
Hir nekke was of good fasoun
In lengthe and gretnesse, by resoun,
Withoute bleyne, scabbe, or royne;
Fro Jerusalem unto Burgoyne
555 Ther nys a fairer nekke, iwys,
To fele how smothe and softe it is;

Hir throte, also whit of hewe
As snowe on braunche snowed newe.
Of body ful wel wrought was she;
560 Men neded not in no cuntre
A fairer body for to seke.

542 **slyke** sleek   551 **fasoun** fashion, shape
553 **bleyne** blemish; **royne** roughness
554 **Burgoyne** Burgundy

The Behaviour of the Courtly Lover

This extract from *The Franklin's Tale* 729–43) describes the wooing
of the ideal courtly lover. This is parodied in different ways in *The
Miller's Tale* in the behaviour of Nicholas and Absolon (163–84,
231–88). Notice the emphasis on the suffering of the lover, on the
great enterprises he undertakes in order to win his love, the lady's
recognition of his worthiness and her pity for his suffering. There is
another admirable description of the behaviour of the lover in *The
Book of the Duchess* (1088–297).

In Armorik, that called is Britayne,
730 Ther was a knyght that loved and dide his payne
To serve a lady in his beste wise;
And many a labour, many a greet emprise,
He for his lady wroghte er she were wonne.
For she was oon the faireste under sonne,
735 And eek therto comen of so heigh kynrede
That wel unnethes dorste this knyght, for drede,
Telle hire his wo, his peyne, and his distresse.
But atte laste she, for his worthynesse,
And namely for his meke obeysaunce,
740 Hath swich a pitee caught of his penaunce
That pryvely she fil of his accord
To take hym for hir housbonde and hir lord,
Of swich lordshipe as men han over hir wyves.

734 **oon the faireste** the fairest   735 **kynrede** family
740 **penaunce** distress, suffering

Two Examples of the Fabliau

The Miller's Tale belongs to the medieval genre of the *fabliau* (described in the Notes on pp. 38–9). The two plot summaries which follow are intended to give a flavour of this unusual genre. *The Butcher of Abbeville* is in some ways a representative *fabliau* with its emphasis on sex and trickery and its low view of human nature (the people in the story will apparently do anything in return for a reward). It is also very characteristic that the priest, who ought to be celibate and charitable to strangers, is depicted as lecherous and materialistic and turns out to be the chief victim of the story.

Plot summary of *The Butcher of Abbeville*

The butcher of Abbeville, returning home from a fruitless journey to the market at Oisemont, asks lodging for the night from the priest of Bailleul. The priest rudely refuses him shelter. On the way out of town he comes upon the priest's sheepfold. The butcher steals one of the sheep and returns to the priest's house, offering to share the meat in return for lodging. The priest agrees, and he and his beautiful mistress enjoy the lamb roast with their guest. When it is time to go to sleep the butcher persuades the priest's serving maid to share his bed in return for the sheepskin. In the morning he finds the priest's mistress alone, and seduces her in return for the promise of the same sheepskin. Well-refreshed he then goes to the church to thank the priest and sells him the sheepskin, which he has left at his house. When he returns home the priest finds his mistress and his serving maid quarrelling over the ownership of the sheepskin he thinks he has just bought. Then his shepherd, who has come to tell him that one of the sheep has been stolen, recognizes the sheepskin. The teller concludes by inviting the audience to debate who has most right to the sheepskin.

(French text in W. Noomen and N. van den Boogaard eds. *Nouveau Receuil Complet des Fabliaux* [Assen, 1982], vol. 3; translation in R. Hellman and R. O'Gorman, *Fabliaux* [London, 1965], pp. 31–44)

Plot summary of *Heile of Beersele*

This is a Flemish *fabliau*, roughly contemporary with *The Miller's Tale*, which combines the same three elements (the misdirected kiss, the second flood, and the branding) to make a somewhat different story. Even if the two stories share a common source, which seems likely, their differences suggest that both poets imposed their own shape on the material as well as (in Chaucer's case) developing character, themes and dialogue. The Flemish version well illustrates the spirit of *fabliau*, while a comparison of the two can reveal how Chaucer adapted the inherited genre to his own purposes.

An Antwerp prostitute named Heile of Beersele once agreed to receive three clients the same night. She arranged for William the Miller to arrive in the early evening, the priest when the sleep-bell rang, and her neighbour the blacksmith at the time of the final curfew. William enjoyed her until the sleep-bell. When the priest arrived she told William to hide in a trough hanging in the rafters. After she and the priest had made love three times, he started to preach to her about a second flood coming to purge the world of its wickedness. When the blacksmith arrived Heile sent him away, saying that she was ill. He was disappointed and begged for a kiss at least. At Heile's suggestion, the priest stuck his bottom out of the window to receive the kiss. When the blacksmith realized the trick that had been played on him, he went to his forge and heated an iron rod. When he returned to the house to beg another kiss, the priest repeated his trick and was rewarded with a scalded bottom. He cried out for water which made William think the second flood had come. He cut his trough down from the rafters, fell to the floor and broke his arm. Running away from William, whom he thought was the devil, the priest fell into the cess-pit and was mocked by the neighbours. The story is told as a warning to those who associate with prostitutes.

(Flemish text and English translation in W. F. Bryan and G. Dempster eds. *Sources and Analogues of Chaucer's Canterbury Tales* [Chicago, 1941], pp. 112–18)